Teaching Reading Comprehension to Students with Learning Difficulties

WHAT WORKS FOR SPECIAL-NEEDS LEARNERS

Karen R. Harris and Steve Graham
Editors

Strategy Instruction for Students with Learning Disabilities
Robert Reid and Torri Ortiz Lienemann

Teaching Mathematics to Middle School Students
with Learning Difficulties
Marjorie Montague and Asha K. Jitendra, Editors

Teaching Word Recognition: Effective Strategies for Teaching Students
with Learning Difficulties
Rollanda E. O'Connor

Teaching Reading Comprehension to Students with Learning Difficulties
Janette K. Klingner, Sharon Vaughn, and Alison Boardman

Teaching Reading Comprehension to Students with Learning Difficulties

Janette K. Klingner
Sharon Vaughn
Alison Boardman

Series Editors' Note by Karen R. Harris and Steve Graham

THE GUILFORD PRESS
New York   London

KH

Library of Congress Cataloging-in-Publication Data

Klingner, Janette K.
  Teaching reading comprehension to students with learning difficulties / Janette K. Klingner,
Sharon Vaughn, Alison Boardman.
      p. cm.—(What works for special-needs learners)
  Includes bibliographical references and index.
  ISBN-13: 978-1-59385-446-1 ISBN-10: 1-59385-446-3 (pbk. : alk. paper)
  ISBN-13: 978-1-59385-447-8 ISBN-10: 1-59385-447-1 (cloth : alk. paper)
  1. Reading comprehension—Study and teaching.   2. Reading—Remedial teaching.
I. Vaughn, Sharon, 1952– II. Boardman, Alison. III. Title.
  LB1050.5.K54 2007
  371.9′04447—dc22

8/25/08

About the Authors

Janette K. Klingner, PhD, is an associate professor at the University of Colorado at Boulder. Before earning her doctorate in reading and learning disabilities from the University of Miami, she was a bilingual special education teacher for 10 years in California and Florida. Dr. Klingner is a co-principal investigator for the National Center for Culturally Responsive Educational Systems, a technical assistance center funded to address the disproportionate representation of culturally and linguistically diverse students in special education, and recently was an investigator for the Center on Personnel Studies in Special Education. To date, she has authored or coauthored 49 journal articles, 9 books (some edited), and 14 book chapters. Dr. Klingner's research interests include reading comprehension strategy instruction for diverse populations, overrepresentation of culturally and linguistically diverse students in special education, and special education teacher quality. She is past Coeditor of the *Review of Educational Research* and an Associate Editor of the *Journal of Learning Disabilities*. In 2004 Dr. Klingner received the American Educational Research Association's Early Career Award for outstanding research.

Sharon Vaughn, PhD, holds the H. E. Hartfelder/Southland Corp. Regents Chair in Human Development at the University of Texas at Austin and has served as the Editor in Chief of the *Journal of Learning Disabilities* and the Coeditor of *Learning Disabilities Research and Practice*. She has received the American Educational Research Association's Special Education Special Interest Group Distinguished Researcher Award and has written numerous books and research articles that address the reading and social outcomes of students with learning difficulties. Dr.

Vaughn is currently the principal investigator or co-principal investigator on several Institute of Education Sciences, National Institute of Child Health and Human Development, and Office of Special Education Programs research grants investigating effective interventions for students with reading difficulties and students who are English language learners.

Alison Boardman, PhD, is an adjunct professor at the University of Colorado at Boulder, where she teaches undergraduate- and graduate-level courses in special education and educational psychology. She works with school districts and state departments across the United States to plan and implement effective professional development in reading. Dr. Boardman is also a consultant for the Vaughn Gross Center for Reading and Language Arts at the University of Texas at Austin, where she is involved in curriculum development, technical assistance, and research for projects that focus on students with reading difficulties. Her research interests include struggling readers, providing effective professional development, and collaboration among general education and special education teachers, and she has published research articles on these topics in leading journals. Dr. Boardman also has many years of experience as a special education teacher in elementary and middle schools.

Series Editors' Note

After their 8-year-old daughter carefully studied the sign in front of Space Mountain at Disney World warning riders about the speed of the rollercoaster, her parents were surprised when she informed them that she would not go on this ride. The year before, she had read the words on the sign out loud, but rode the rollercoaster repeatedly and talked about nothing else for days. Even though her parents encouraged her to go with her brothers and sisters, she steadfastly refused, declaring, "This year, I know what the words on the sign say!"

This story illustrates a simple but powerful fact—reading the words correctly is not enough; you have to understand what they say. In fact, you not only need to understand what they say but also must be able to go beyond the literal meaning of the text, think critically about the message, appreciate what the author is trying to say, and understand when you do not understand. Unfortunately, too many children experience difficulty mastering these fundamental reading processes and skills. *Teaching Reading Comprehension to Students with Learning Difficulties* by Janette K. Klingner, Sharon Vaughn, and Alison Boardman tackles this problem head on by providing teachers and other practitioners with validated instructional techniques for teaching reading comprehension to students with learning difficulties.

This book is part of the What Works for Special-Needs Learners series. This series addresses a significant need in the education of students who are at risk, those with disabilities, and all children and adolescents who struggle with learning or behavior. Researchers in special education, educational psychology, curriculum and instruction, and other fields have made great progress in understanding what works for struggling learners, yet the practical application of this research base remains quite limited. This is due in part to the lack of appropriate materials for teachers, teacher educators, and inservice teacher development programs. Books in this series present assessment, instructional, and classroom management methods with a strong research base and provide specific "how-to" instructions and examples of the use of proven procedures in schools.

Teaching Reading Comprehension to Students with Learning Difficulties presents instructional techniques and activities that are scientifically validated, moving from how to assess reading comprehension to teaching students how to flexibly and effectively use multiple comprehension strategies. These evidence-based practices provide teachers with the tools they need to ensure that all of their students master the process involved in understanding, evaluating, appreciating, and acquiring new knowledge from what they read. An invaluable resource for practitioners, this book is also suitable for use in reading methods courses and coursework in the area of learning disabilities and reading disabilities.

Future books in the series will cover such issues as vocabulary instruction, self-determination, social skills instruction, writing, working with families, academic instruction for students with behavioral difficulties, and more. All volumes will be as thorough and detailed as the present one and will facilitate implementation of evidence-based practices in classrooms and schools.

KAREN R. HARRIS
STEVE GRAHAM

Preface

Wen reading is effortless, which is likely the case for those reading this preface, it is difficult to imagine what it might be like to read print and not be able to understand it or say much about it afterward. Although we might occasionally encounter text with which we are unfamiliar or in which we are uninterested and therefore have reduced comprehension, it is difficult for us to imagine what it would be like to experience these same challenges with *all* material that we read. Yet, we have all taught many students who lack understanding of whatever they read, and we struggle with ways to increase their reading and comprehension skills.

This book is for all teachers who teach students who struggle with understanding and learning from text. We envision that teachers will use this book to help students develop a love for the "world of imagination" as well as for the learning through text that can happen only when they truly comprehend what they read. From a very early age, children enjoy listening to books being read by others and discussing what they think might happen next or how a story connects to their lives. In these early phases they acquire important strategies and develop competencies that will help them with reading comprehension later. Even in the primary grades, when students are learning how to identify words and are developing basic reading skills, teachers also attend to their students' reading comprehension. As students develop proficiency with basic reading skills, teachers shift their emphasis to helping students develop reading comprehension strategies and become increasingly sophisticated readers of a variety of texts for a multitude of purposes.

The comprehension practices described in this book provide effective instruction to *all* students, including those who require additional support. Increasing demands for accountability and pressure to improve academic achievement for all students, including students with learning disabilities, require that teachers be even more knowledgeable and skillful to meet the increasing needs of a range of learners. And as the laws that govern special education increasingly call for instruction to take place in the general education setting, classrooms are becoming more heterogeneous. We view this increased scrutiny of the success of typically underachieving students as an opportunity for teachers to exercise their best teaching, resulting in improved outcomes for all students.

In this book we focus on methods for teaching reading comprehension to students with learning disabilities and reading difficulties, with special emphasis on those practices that are supported by research. We provide descriptions of the knowledge base in each of the critical areas related to comprehension and also present specific strategies for teachers to implement with their students.

ORGANIZATION OF THE BOOK

In Chapter 1 we provide an overview of reading comprehension as a domain of learning. This chapter is meant to serve as a backdrop for the assessment and methods chapters that follow. We provide a summary of current research on effective practices for improving reading comprehension for students with learning difficulties and disabilities. We describe how good and poor readers differ in their reading comprehension and the strategies good readers use to facilitate their understanding. We discuss possible reasons students with learning disabilities might struggle with reading comprehension, and we describe the cognitive processes involved in comprehension.

In Chapter 2 we review various reading comprehension assessment procedures that teachers can use either diagnostically or for progress monitoring purposes. We describe standardized tests, curriculum-based measurement, informal reading inventories, interviews and questionnaires, observations, retelling, and think-aloud procedures. We emphasize that it is important for those administering different comprehension measures to be aware of just what each test assesses, what can and cannot be learned, and the limitations as well as the strengths of each. The best way to assess reading comprehension is with a combination of different measures.

In Chapter 3 we describe ways to enhance vocabulary instruction. Understanding words in all their complexity is an essential part of comprehending text. Many students with learning disabilities have less extensive vocabularies than their peers without disabilities. Numerous factors contribute to differential rates of vocabulary growth. Some students with disabilities suffer from general language deficits that affect their vocabulary learning, and others have problems with memory and/or recall. We describe numerous instructional methods, designed to improve vocabulary learning, which have helped students with learning disabilities and other struggling readers.

In Chapter 4 we discuss the importance of understanding text structure and present multiple ways to teach students about different narrative and expository text structures. Although students with learning disabilities and other students are often unaware of, or confused by, unfamiliar text structures, explicit instruction can help them recognize various structures and use this knowledge to aid their comprehension. This principle applies to students at different grade levels, from the primary grades through high school.

In Chapter 5 we describe specific instructional practices that promote reading comprehension. We organize these comprehension strategies in terms of when they are typically used: before, during, and after reading. Prior to reading, teachers should assist students in activating, building, and using their background knowledge to make connections with the text and predict what they will learn. During reading, students need to know how to monitor their understanding, use fix-up strategies to assist with comprehension, and consider linkages between what they are reading and previous knowledge and experiences. After reading, they should summarize the key ideas they have read and respond to the material in various ways.

Finally, in Chapter 6 we discuss multicomponent approaches to strategy instruction, including reciprocal teaching, transactional strategies instruction, and collaborative strategic reading. With each approach students learn to apply different strategies through modeling, explicit instruction, and guided practice, before, during, and after reading. Each approach includes discussions with peers as a central element. These methods have been found to be effective for improving the reading comprehension of students with learning disabilities as well as other students.

FEATURES

This book includes many features designed to make it readily accessible to educators. In each chapter we provide background information about the research supporting the aspect of reading comprehension under discussion. We also describe how to carry out different instructional approaches and utilize numerous figures, graphs, and tables to illustrate our approaches. In selected chapters we also offer sample lesson plans. Finally, at the beginning of each chapter we list three or four study group questions designed to prompt reflection and dialogue about reading comprehension. This book is designed to help undergraduate and graduate students extend their knowledge of reading instruction related to comprehension as well as to assist practicing teachers in furthering their expertise.

USING THIS BOOK AS A STUDY GUIDE

We encourage you to use this book as a study guide in your school. Whether you are part of a formal study group or would like to start your own informal group, this book can serve as a valuable tool to guide your pedagogy. Much like the interactive comprehension practices associated with improved outcomes for students, we believe that educators who have opportunities to discuss and implement ideas from this book with feedback from their fellow teachers are more likely to try the comprehension practices and maintain their use.

ACKNOWLEDGMENTS

We have many to acknowledge but feel compelled to select just a few. Janette Klingner would like to recognize and express appreciation for the guidance of two experts in reading comprehension: the late Michael Pressley and Annmarie Palincsar. I first met them in 1992 when, as a naive yet eager doctoral student, I approached each of them at an annual meeting of the National Reading Conference and asked if they would be willing to serve as consultants on a student-initiated research grant (for my dissertation). They both graciously agreed and over the years have been very generous with their time, expertise, and wisdom. I have learned much not only about reading comprehension but also about life. For this guidance, I am very grateful.

Sharon Vaughn would like to acknowledge the contributions of Isabel Beck and Jean Osborn. Isabel Beck is simply the most insightful and interesting person with whom I have dialogued about reading. She is enormously interested in my research, my thinking, my interpretations. She is also exceedingly generous with what she knows—and she knows a lot. She has not hesitated to "set me straight," and she has always been right. Jean Osborn and I have worked closely together on professional development materials for the past 9 years. She is vigorous, dedicated, exacting, and sensitive. She wears me out with her precise rejuvenation of tired writing. She knows what teachers need to know and do to assure that all students read well, often, and with enthusiasm. I simply have no words for how much I have learned from her about teaching, learning, and caring for others. I appreciate most that Isabel and Jean are my friends.

We all remember students who, despite their inquisitive minds, lack the skills they need to learn from reading and, perhaps even worse, might never have the chance to love to read. Alison Boardman would like to acknowledge these students (and their teachers), who continually encourage her to become a better educator because they simply wouldn't have it any other way. I would also like to thank my coauthors, Janette Klingner and Sharon Vaughn, whose expertise and longstanding commitment to the field is inspirational. Their feedback and support have been invaluable to me.

Contents

CHAPTER 1

Overview of Reading Comprehension

STUDY GROUP PROMPTS

1. How do good and poor readers differ when they talk about text they have read? Can you determine from students' responses to text whether they really understood what they read?

2. If students with learning difficulties/disabilities have trouble with reading comprehension, what are the possible explanations? Are there other factors related to reading comprehension that might need to be considered?

3. Reading comprehension is difficult to determine in students because so much of it occurs "in the head" and isn't readily observable. What can you do to better determine how well your students understand what they read?

How is it that children learn to understand what they read? How do some students get lost in their reading and enter new worlds, build knowledge, and improve vocabulary, whereas others find reading a constant struggle that rarely nets comprehension? As teachers of students with reading difficulties and disabilities, these questions were asked anew each year with each incoming group of students. Few of the students we taught who had learning disabilities also read well and with comprehension. In this chapter we present an overview of reading comprehension and related factors.

1

Meaning, learning, and pleasure are the ultimate goals of learning to read. Although fundamental skills such as phonics and fluency are important building blocks of reading, reading comprehension is the "sine qua non of reading" (Beck & McKeown, 1998). Knowing how to read words has ultimately little value if the student is unable to construct meaning from text. Ultimately, reading comprehension is the process of constructing meaning by coordinating a number of complex processes that include word reading, word and world knowledge, and fluency (Anderson, Hiebert, Scott, & Wilkinson, 1985; Jenkins, Larson, & Fleischer, 1983; O'Shea, Sindelar, & O'Shea, 1987).

In the last few years the phonological awareness and decoding skills of students with reading disabilities have been identified as serious inhibitors to successful reading (Ball & Blachman, 1991; O'Connor & Jenkins, 1995; Vellutino & Scanlon, 1987). Although there is little question that difficulties in these foundational skills impede successful growth in reading for many students, it is also true that many students with learning disabilities have significant challenges understanding and learning from text even when they are able to decode adequately (Williams, 1998, 2000). Explicit and highly structured development of beginning reading skills is required, as is highly structured instruction in reading comprehension (Gersten & Carnine, 1986; Gersten, Fuchs, Williams, & Baker, 2001).

In a landmark reading study, Durkin (1978–1979) conducted an observational study of reading comprehension instruction. She revealed that typical comprehension instruction wasn't very engaging or likely to improve reading comprehension. She summarized reading comprehension instruction as following a three-step procedure: mentioning, practicing, and assessing. That is, teachers would *mention* the skill that they wanted students to use, then they would give them opportunities to *practice* that skill through workbooks or skill sheets, and finally *assess* whether or not they used the skill successfully. Instruction was noticeably missing. Perhaps of even greater concern than the quality of comprehension instruction was the dearth of reading instruction observed. Based on more than 4,000 minutes of reading instruction observed in fourth-grade classrooms, only 20 minutes of comprehension instruction was recorded. This study significantly influenced research in reading comprehension (Dole, Duffy, Roehler, & Pearson, 1991). However, subsequent observation studies revealed little influence on classroom practice (Pressley & El-Dinary, 1997; Schumm, Moody, & Vaughn, 2000; Vaughn, Moody, & Schumm, 1998).

In an attempt to improve comprehension instruction, several theories have been proposed that suggest ways to influence understanding of the teaching of reading comprehension: schema theory, reader-response theory, and direct instruction. A brief description of each of these influential theories provides the background for interpreting the instructional practices related to teaching reading comprehension that are presented in more detail elsewhere in this book.

Schema theory suggests that what we know about a topic or construct influences how much we can or will learn by reading a passage that addresses that topic

(Anderson & Pearson, 1984). Thus our knowledge and experiences related to key ideas in the text we read influence what we learn and remember about what we read. World knowledge and word meaning influence our understanding. The more we read and learn about the topic, the easier the next passage on that topic will be for us to understand.

From a reader-response constructivist perspective (Beach, 1993), understanding what is read is related to the individual's experiences and interpretations of these experiences. This subjective component makes for a dynamic interaction between the reader and the text. Thus, what readers learn or how they respond to text is individualistic. Teachers and peers can facilitate and interact with other readers to enhance and extend learning.

Direct instruction approaches have been associated with improved outcomes in reading comprehension for students with learning disabilities (Darch & Kame'enui, 1987; Lloyd, Cullinan, Heins, & Epstein, 1980; Polloway, Epstein, Polloway, Patton, & Ball, 1986; Stein & Goldman, 1980). Direct instruction approaches provide for more explicit and systematic instruction related to the key ideas associated with improved reading comprehension. For example, because word meaning relates to understanding text, a direct instruction approach would ask teachers to identify key words in a passage and teach their meaning prior to reading.

WHAT DO GOOD AND POOR READERS DO RELATED TO READING COMPREHENSION?

Many of the instructional practices suggested for poor readers were derived from observing, questioning, and asking good and poor readers to "think aloud" while they read (Dole et al., 1991; Heilman, Blair, & Rupley, 1998; Jiménez, Garcia, & Pearson, 1995, 1996). Reports of how good readers understand and learn from text suggest that they coordinate a set of highly complex and well-developed skills and strategies before, during, and after reading that assist them in understanding and remembering what they read (Paris, Wasik, & Tumer, 1991). Perhaps the most succinct way to characterize good readers is to say that they are more strategic than poor readers (Paris, Lipson, & Wixson, 1983). The skills and strategies that good readers use include:

- Rapid and accurate word reading
- Setting goals for reading
- Noting the structure and organization of text
- Monitoring their understanding while reading
- Creating mental notes and summaries
- Making predictions about what will happen, checking them as they go along, and revising and evaluating them as needed

- Capitalizing on what they know about the topic and integrating that with new learning
- Making inferences
- Using mental images such as visualization to assist them in remembering or understanding events or characters

In addition, good bilingual readers are able to draw upon their translation skills, knowledge of cognates, and ability to transfer information across languages to a much greater extent than struggling readers (Jiménez et al., 1996). These strategies appear to be unique to bilingual reading.

In contrast with the integrated and strategic approaches to understanding text applied by good readers, poor readers use few effective strategies for understanding and remembering what they read (Pressley & Afflerbach, 1995). They are often less interested in reading, their motivation is often low, they prepare minimally, if at all, prior to reading, they use few metacognitive strategies to monitor their learning from text, and they have inadequate vocabulary and background knowledge with which to connect and link new ideas to previous learning. Furthermore, unlike good readers, poor readers lack the decoding, word reading, and fluency skills to free up cognitive functioning so that their full attention can be focused on learning from reading.

Students with learning disabilities are often the poorest readers; they demonstrate multiple problems associated with low comprehension, including poor decoding, fluency, and comprehension. These students also exhibit characteristics of inactive learners (Torgesen & Licht, 1983) who do not monitor their learning or use strategies effectively. Yet, students with learning disabilities can improve their reading comprehension if teachers:

1. Teach strategies that have been documented as effective in promoting reading comprehension.
2. Design instruction that incorporates effective principles of direct instruction and strategy instruction.
3. Provide modeling, support, guided instruction, practice, attributional feedback, and opportunities to practice across text types.
4. Monitor students' progress and make adjustments accordingly (Mastropieri & Scruggs, 1997).

Many of the reading comprehension strategies that have been associated with the highest effect sizes for students with learning disabilities are those that teach students strategies that prompt them to monitor and reflect before, during, and after reading. These strategies ask students to (1) consider their background knowledge on the topic they are reading, (2) summarize key ideas, and (3) self-question while they read (e.g., Gersten et al., 2001; Jenkins, Heliotis, Stein, & Haynes, 1987; Mastropieri, Scruggs, Bakken, & Whedon, 1996; Swanson, 1999; Wong & Jones, 1982) (see Figure 1.1).

Direct instruction, strategy instruction, or a combination of both are associated with the highest effect sizes in reading comprehension for students with learning disabilities. Both direct instruction and strategy instruction have the following components in common:

1. Assessment and evaluation of learning objectives, including orienting students to what they will be learning
2. Daily reviews of material taught to assure mastery
3. Teacher presentation of new material, including giving examples and demonstrating what students need to do
4. Guided instruction, including asking questions to determine understanding
5. Feedback and correction
6. Independent practice and review

The instructional components that contribute the most to improved effect sizes in reading comprehension include:

1. Teacher and students questioning
2. Interactive dialogue between teachers and students and students and students
3. Controlling task difficulty and scaffolding instruction
4. Elaboration of steps or strategies and modeling by the teacher
5. Small group instruction
6. Use of cues to help students remember to use and apply what they learn

FIGURE 1.1. Key ideas in reading comprehension. Information in this figure is adapted from work conducted by Swanson and colleagues (Swanson, 1999, 2001; Swanson, Hoskyn, & Lee, 1999).

TO WHAT DEGREE DO THE FOUNDATIONAL SKILLS OF PHONICS, FLUENCY, AND VOCABULARY INFLUENCE READING COMPREHENSION?

Students with learning disabilities are likely to demonstrate difficulties with decoding, fluency (reading words quickly and accurately), and vocabulary. Difficulty in any of these three areas will interfere with reading comprehension. One reason for this interference is that readers only have so much short-term cognitive, or thinking, capacity for a task. If too much effort is allocated to decoding, little capacity is available for focusing on comprehension.

Myra, Laticia, and Jorge are sixth-grade students identified with learning disabilities who demonstrate significant problems understanding text. Myra has difficulty reading multisyllabic words and still confuses basic sight words such as *from*, *where*, and *laugh*. Although she has difficulty with decoding, Myra is very interested in many topics related to social justice and is motivated to read and learn. Her difficulties decoding words slow down her reading and often require her to read slowly and to reread text in order to understand it. Myra's text reading improves when key words are reviewed and taught to her prior to reading. Laticia, though an accurate word reader, reads very slowly (about 60 correct words per minute). This slow reading negatively influences comprehension and also makes it difficult for her to read widely. Jorge reads quickly as long as he is very familiar with the words. Jorge's problem is that he does not know the meanings of many words that appear in his expository text for science and social studies. Because he does not enjoy reading, he does not read often, and thus his knowledge of new words and ideas is limited. His very limited vocabulary and world knowledge prevent him from fully understanding what he has read because he either lacks sufficient background knowledge or misses the meaning of so many words that comprehension on all but a superficial level is difficult.

Myra, Laticia, and Jorge provide examples of the difficulties that many students with learning disabilities have with reading comprehension and illustrate the value of teaching critical foundational skills such as word reading (decoding), fluency (accuracy and speed of reading), vocabulary (knowing what the words mean in context), and world knowledge (having sufficient background knowledge to benefit from reading text). Many students with learning disabilities have problems in more than one area that influence their text comprehension. Teachers who are aware of the many elements that contribute to comprehension are more likely to consider these when assessing students' reading comprehension difficulties and implementing targeted instruction.

What Can Teachers Do If Older Students Have Poor Word Reading (Decoding)?

Knowing how to read, or decode, words is not a small part of the reading process—it is a critical link whose absence inhibits understanding. When students are beginning to read, they may have difficulty with such words as *saw*, *them*, and *their*. As students progress through reading, they may have difficulty reading such words as *challenge*, *fascinate*, and *immune*. The goal is to identify, prior to reading, the key words that students are likely to have challenges decoding and teaching them so that students can read these words and use them in discussions and written expression. Achieving this goal with students with learning disabilities is no easy matter.

Teachers can provide support by teaching the decoding skills students need initially to read more basic words. After students can read basic words and have the fundamental phonics principles to decode words, then teachers need to provide instruction in the decoding of more complex and multisyllabic words. A few pointers to facilitate decoding in older students include the following:

• Practice decoding with very complicated, multisyllabic words. Break these words into syllables and then treat each syllable as a separate word type for decoding.

• Ask students to locate words that they cannot read. Keep these words in a word bank or on a word wall and use them for activities on teaching decoding.

• Teach students common rules for decoding and remind them to use these rules when reading multisyllabic words. Review rules using key words from the text. For example, in the word *reduction*, show students that there are three word parts: *re duc tion*. Use the rules students know and the words they currently can read to help them decode each word part and then read the entire word.

- Teach students common prefixes, suffixes, and affixes so that reading multi-syllabic words is easier and more meaningful.
- Demonstrate that some words are "irregular" and do not meet the typical rules of our language. Keep a word wall of irregular words that students need to practice.
- Indicate that proper nouns, such as the names of people, places, and things, are often difficult to read. Learning what these names refer to in the chapter before reading and connecting them, so that students know who the story is about, where it takes place, and other related issues, facilitate word reading and comprehension.

Beck's (2006) multisyllabic word strategy is highly appropriate for older readers. Students can learn to read and remember difficult words by selecting syllables from each of three columns to build multisyllabic words. For example, students can have a list of eight syllables in column 1, eight syllables in column 2, and eight syllables in column 3, and figure out how to select and combine them to make complex words. For example, the syllables *fre*, *quent*, and *ly* are combined to make *frequently*. The syllables *in*, *fec*, and *tion* are combined to make *infection*. Figure 1.2 provides a list of resources to assist with teaching decoding.

What Can Teachers Do If Students Have Poor Fluency?

Reading words quickly and accurately allows students to "free up" their thinking so that they can concentrate on text meaning (Perfetti, 1985; Perfetti & Lesgold, 1977). Reading slowly is a problem for two reasons: (1) It keeps students from reading enough text to keep up with class expectations; and (2) it prevents students

---

Building Words: A Resource Manual for Teaching Word Analysis and Spelling Strategies (2001) by T. G. Gunning. Boston: Allyn & Bacon.

- *Making Sense of Phonics: The Hows and Whys* (2006) by I. L. Beck. New York: Guilford Press.
- *Phonics from A to Z: A Practical Guide* (2nd ed.) (2006) by W. Blevins. New York: Scholastic Professional Books.
- *Phonics They Use: Words for Reading and Writing* (2004) by P. Cunningham. New York: Longman.
- *Word Journeys: Assessment-Guided Phonics, Spelling, and Vocabulary Instruction* (2000) by K. Ganske. New York: Guilford Press.
- *Words Their Way: Word Study for Phonics, Vocabulary, and Spelling Instruction* (3rd ed.) (2003) by D. R. Bear, M. Invernizzi, S. R. Templeton, & F. Johnston. Upper Saddle River, NJ: Prentice Hall.
- *Teaching Word Recognition: Effective Strategies for Students with Learning Difficulties* (2007) by R. E. O'Connor. New York: Guilford Press.

FIGURE 1.2. Resources for teaching decoding.

from adequately remembering what they read. You can imagine how reading very slowing and laboriously might discourage students and reduce interest in reading and learning from print.

How fast should students read? Students need to read between 100 and 150 words correct per minute if they want to read at the average pace for students in the middle grades (Hasbrouck & Tindal, 1992). To achieve this goal, students need to know how to read words automatically, without a lot of pauses to decode.

Teachers can provide support by teaching fluency skills students need to read for comprehension. A few pointers to facilitate fluency include the following:

- Monitor students' progress in reading by asking them to read information passages at the grade level you are teaching. Calculate the correct words read per minute. Ask students to monitor their progress by graphing results.
- Ask students to reread difficult passages.
- Ask students to work with peer partners to read and reread passages.
- Identify key words and proper nouns and preteach prior to asking students to read text.
- Students' fluency increases when they listen to books or text on tape prior to reading independently.
- Give opportunities for students to showcase their reading by asking them to prepare a passage or dialogue to read aloud to the class. Advanced preparation allows students time to read and reread material—an effective practice for improving fluency.
- Names of people, places, and things are often difficult to read; teach these prior to reading.

Figure 1.3 provides a list of resources to assist with teaching fluency.

WHAT IS INVOLVED IN READING COMPREHENSION?

Reading comprehension involves much more than readers' responses to text. Reading comprehension is a multicomponent, highly complex process that involves many interactions between readers and what they bring to the text (previous knowledge, strategy use) as well as variables related to the text itself (interest in text, understanding of text types).

Cognitive Processes

What is actually happening when we comprehend what we are reading? Irwin (1991) describes five basic comprehension processes that work together simultaneously and complement one another: microprocesses, integrative processes, macroprocesses, elaborative processes, and metacognitive processes. We describe

Peer-Assisted Learning Strategies—Reading (PALS) (Classwide Peer Tutoring)
Contact: PALS Outreach
Vanderbilt University
Peabody Box 328
230 Appleton Place
Nashville, TN 37203-5701
Website: *kc.vanderbilt.edu/pals*

Read Naturally
Contact: Read Naturally
750 South Plaza Drive, #100
Saint Paul, MN 55120
Website: *www.readnaturally.com*

Great Leaps
Contact: Diamuid, Inc.
Box 357580
Gainesville, FL 32636
Website: *www.greatleaps.com*

First Grade PALS (Peer-Assisted Literacy Strategies)
Contact: Sopris West
4093 Specialty Place
Longwood, CO 80504-5400
Website: *www.sopriswest.com*

Quick Reads: A Research-Based Fluency Program
Contact: Modern Curriculum Press
299 Jefferson Road
Parsippany, NJ 07054
Website: *www.pearsonlearning.com*

FIGURE 1.3. Resources for teaching fluency.

each of these next (also, see Figure 1.4). While reading about these different cognitive processes, keep in mind that the reader uses these different strategies fluidly, going back and forth from focusing on specific chunks of text, as with microprocessing, to stepping back and reflecting about what has been read, as with metacognition.

Microprocesses

Microprocessing refers to the reader's initial chunking of idea units within individual sentences. "Chunking" involves grouping words into phrases or clusters of words that carry meaning, and requires an understanding of syntax as well as vocabulary. For example, consider the following sentence:

Michelle put the yellow roses in a vase.

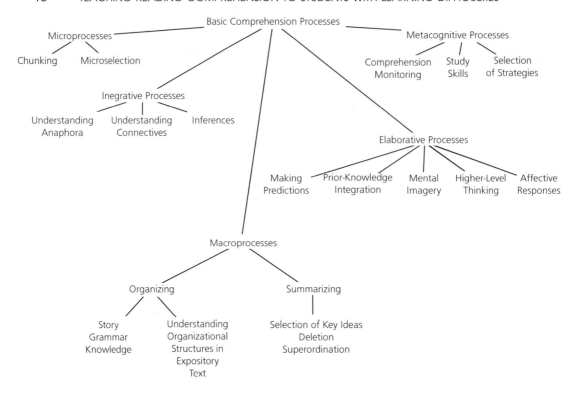

FIGURE 1.4. Irwin's five basic comprehension processes. Adapted from Irwin (1991). Copyright 1991 by Pearson Education. Adapted by permission.

The reader does not picture *yellow* and *roses* separately, but instead immediately visualizes roses that are the color yellow. The good reader processes *yellow roses* together.

Selective recall is another aspect of microprocessing. The reader must decide which chunks of text or which details are important to remember. When reading only one sentence, it is relatively easy to recall details, but remembering becomes more difficult after reading a long passage. For example, the reader may or may not remember later that the roses were yellow. To some extent, whether this detail is remembered will depend upon its significance in the passage. In other words, does it matter in the story that the roses were yellow, or is this just an unimportant detail?

Integrative Processes

As the reader progresses through individual sentences, he or she is processing more than the individual meaning units within sentences. He or she is also actively making connections across sentences. This process of understanding and inferring the relationships among clauses is referred to as integrative processing. Subskills involved in integrative processing include being able to identify and understand pronoun referents and being able to infer causation or sequence. The following two sentences demonstrate how these subskills are applied:

Michael quickly locked the door and shut the windows.
He was afraid.

To whom does *he* apply? Good readers seem to automatically know that *he* in the second sentence refers to *Michael* in the first sentence. And good readers infer that Michael locked the door and shut the windows *because* he was afraid.

Macroprocesses

Ideas are better understood and more easily remembered when the reader is able to organize them in a coherent way. The reader does this by summarizing the key ideas read. He or she may either automatically or deliberately (i.e., subconsciously or consciously) select the most important information to remember and delete relatively less important details. The skillful reader also uses a structure or organizational pattern to help him or her organize these important ideas. More proficient comprehenders know to use the same organizational pattern provided by the author to organize their ideas (e.g., a story map that includes characters and setting/problem/solution in a narrative or a compare-and-contrast text structure for an expository passage).

Elaborative Processes

When we read, we tap into our prior knowledge and make inferences beyond points described explicitly in the text. We make inferences that may or may not correspond with those intended by the author. For instance, in the two sentences provided above about Michael, we do not know why he was afraid. But we can predict that perhaps he was worried that someone had followed him home, or maybe a storm was brewing and he was concerned about strong winds. When making these inferences, we may draw upon information provided earlier in the text or upon our own previous experiences (e.g., perhaps at some point the reader was followed home and hurried inside and quickly shut and locked the door). This process is called elaborative processing.

Metacognitive Processes

Much has been made of the importance of metacognition, that is, thinking about thinking. Metacognition is the reader's conscious awareness or control of cognitive processes. The metacognitive processes the reader uses are those involved in monitoring understanding, selecting what to remember, and regulating the strategies used when reading. The metacognitive strategies the reader uses include rehears-

ing (i.e., repeating information to enhance recall), reviewing, underlining important words or sections of a passage, note taking, and checking understanding.

CONCLUSION

In this book we provide an overview of instructional practices and assessments for
reading comprehension that can be used to enhance reading comprehension outcomes for students with learning difficulties and disabilities. This book is intended
for general and special education teachers interested in assessing and intervening
with students at risk for reading difficulties. We provide an up-to-date summary of
what we have learned, as a field, from research on the reading comprehension of
students with learning disabilities. We know that reading comprehension is a complex process of constructing meaning by coordinating a number of skills related to
decoding, word reading, and fluency (Jenkins, Larson, & Fleischer, 1983; O'Shea,
Sindelar, & O'Shea, 1987) and the integration of background knowledge, vocabulary, and previous experiences (Anderson et al., 1985). Most notably, "Comprehension is an active process to which the reader brings his or her individual attitudes,
interests, [and] expectations" (Irwin, 1991, p. 7).

CHAPTER 2

Assessing Reading Comprehension

STUDY GROUP PROMPTS

1. Before reading this chapter, think about what you already know about
   assessing students' reading comprehension. What are the different tests or
   procedures you use? Ask members of your study group how they are
   currently assessing reading comprehension.

2. As you read, think about which assessment procedures you already implement with your students. Do the procedures you are currently using tap into
   different levels of comprehension? Do they yield an accurate portrayal of
   students' reading comprehension?

3. After reading this chapter, discuss with your study group what you learned
   about different ways to assess students' reading comprehension. What comprehension assessment tests and procedures might you add to your repertoire, and why?

TEACHER: When I give you this to read, what is the first thing you do?

STUDENT 1: I guess what it is going to be about. I predict. I read the title and then I
start reading. Sometimes I look at the pictures to help predict, and the title, and
the map, and things to help. (*reading*) "About 25 years ago, logging companies
began cutting rainforest trees on Borneo. The loggers call the trees 'green gold'
because the trees are worth so much money. They cut the trees to make paper,
chopsticks, and other products."

TEACHER: What are you thinking?

STUDENT 1: That the people that are cutting them are so selfish because they think that once they cut down the trees they are going to get a lot of money and they are going to cut those trees for wood, paper, chopstick, and "firewoods" and things that kill the trees.

TEACHER: Anything else?

STUDENT 1: And the people don't care; they are ruining the rainforest and all they want is the money and they don't care about the people who live there—they want to get trees. (*reading*) "The people are the Penan. They live in an ancient rainforest on Borneo, an island near Asia. They live by gathering fruits, nuts, and roots, and by hunting. The Penan way of life, along with the rainforest, is being destroyed. 'I just want to cry when I hear the bulldozers and saws,' says Juwin Lihan, a Penan leader."

TEACHER: What are you thinking?

STUDENT 2: That they are saying that they don't like the sound of bulldozers, saws, or anything that cuts trees and—they told them to stop and that it is happening and that they don't. Most of the rainforest is going to be destroyed. They are going to kill all the animals that live there and leave their habitat and maybe they will kill thousands and hundreds of baby animals that are extinct like the grey wolves. I don't know if they are extinct, and rhinoceros and other animals.

TEACHER: What do you do when you do not understand a word or an idea the first time you read it?

STUDENT 2: I use the clunk strategies we have in CSR [collaborative strategic reading]. First, we read the sentence without the word and second, we read the sentence before and after the clunk looking for clues . . . We find the prefix and suffix. Finally, we would break the word apart into smaller parts to help us know what the meaning of the word is. . . .

—Excerpts from the responses of two fourth-grade students with learning disabilities to the "Prompted Think-Aloud" (Klingner et al., 2004; see Appendix 2.1)

In this chapter we describe how to assess the reading comprehension of students with learning disabilities (LD). Assessing comprehension is fraught with challenges, because it can be difficult to determine how much students really know and what they are actually thinking (as we attempted to do in the preceding example). Traditional measures tend to focus on straight recall or literal understandings, but there is much more to comprehension than these.

Reading comprehension assessment has different purposes. One of these is to compare students' comprehension levels to those of students in a norming sample. Another is to find out if students have met preestablished criteria for their grade level. A third purpose is to inform instruction by determining when students understand what they read and how efficiently they use which comprehension strategies. Similarly, an important purpose is determining why a student may be struggling. Teachers must be adept at collecting assessment data so that they can plan what, how, and when to teach (Haager & Klingner, 2005). The types of assessment materials and activities the teacher (or other examiner) uses should be determined by the purpose of the assessment. If we know what type of information we need, we can decide what process to follow. As Salvia and Ysseldyke suggest, we should not talk about assessment unless we talk about "*assessment for the purpose of . . .* " (2001, p. 5).

In this chapter we first discuss the limitations of traditional approaches to assessing comprehension. We then describe various traditional as well as innovative reading comprehension assessment measures, including standardized norm-referenced tests, criterion-referenced tests, informal reading inventories, curriculum-based assessment, curriculum-based measurement, interviews and questionnaires, anecdotal records and observations, oral retelling, and think-aloud procedures (e.g., as illustrated at the beginning of this chapter). For each technique we describe its purpose, how it is implemented, and its relative strengths and weaknesses. We finish the chapter with a checklist for teachers to use to evaluate their comprehension instruction.

LIMITATIONS OF TRADITIONAL COMPREHENSION ASSESSMENT PROCEDURES

Traditional measures of reading comprehension are limited in that they provide only a general indicator of how well a student understands text, and they are not based on experts' knowledge of what good readers do to comprehend text. It is generally agreed that good readers connect new text with past experiences, interpret, evaluate, synthesize, and consider alternative interpretations of what they have read (Pressley & Afflerbach, 1995). Good readers are able to monitor their understanding and use all available information while attempting to make sense of the text (Baker, 2002; Flavell, 1979; Mokhtari & Reichard, 2002; Pressley, 2000). The reader's response to text is quite personal (Rosenblatt, 1983) and varies depending on a number of factors, including (but not limited to) interest, background knowledge, purpose for reading, and characteristics of the text.

Despite views of reading as an interactive, reflective process, however, reading comprehension measures generally focus on recall as the primary indicator of students' understanding (Applegate, Quinn, & Applegate, 2002). Comprehension is typically measured by requiring students to read a short passage and then answer multiple-choice or short-answer questions or by using a cloze task (i.e., asking students to fill in blanks where words have been omitted; Irwin, 1991). These traditional measures of reading comprehension provide only a basic indication of how well a student understands text and offer little information about how the student uses cognitive and metacognitive processes. In short, they do not explain *why* a student may be struggling. Nor do they help us detect and diagnose specific comprehension problems. As bluntly noted by Snow (2002), "Widely used comprehension assessments are inadequate" (p. 52). Clearly, better standardized measures are needed, as well as innovative procedures that evaluate aspects of comprehension not assessed by standardized instruments (Kamhi, 1997). Teachers should have a repertoire of options at their fingertips. In Table 2.1 we list limitations of commonly used measures as well as promising practices for improving the assessment process.

In summary, missing from most reading comprehension measures is a link between information obtained from the measure and reading instruction. What we learn from most comprehension measures is how students are performing, not

TABLE 2.1. Limitations of Commonly Used Comprehension Measures versus Promising Practices

Drawbacks of commonly used measures	Promising assessment practices
• Not based on a current theory of reading comprehension	• Reflect authentic outcomes
• Not based on an understanding of reading comprehension as a developmental process or as an outcome of instruction	• Better reflect the dynamic, developmental nature of comprehension
• Tend to be one-dimensional and narrow	• Provide information about how individuals perform across activities with varying purposes and with a variety of texts and text types
• Tend to focus on immediate recall and fail to capture the complexity of reading comprehension	• Identify individual children as weak comprehenders as well as subtypes of weak comprehenders
• Conflate or confuse comprehension with vocabulary, background knowledge, word reading ability, and other reading skills and capacities	• Capture the interactions among the dimensions of reader, activity, text, and context
• Do not provide information that is useful for diagnostic or planning purposes	• Inform instruction (provide useful information about strengths and weaknesses for planning purposes)
• Lack adequate reliability and validity	• Adaptable with respect to individual, social, linguistic, and cultural variations

Note. Adapted from Snow (2002). Copyright 2002 by the RAND Corporation. Adapted by permission.

what instruction would improve their reading comprehension. In the next section we describe different assessment tools.

READING COMPREHENSION MEASURES

A wide range of assessment instruments and procedures is available (see Table 2.2). When selecting a test or assessment procedure to use with students with LD, it is important to select the measure that most closely matches the users' needs or purpose. Uses of available reading comprehension assessments typically range from determining a student's reading comprehension competence relative to a normative group, to determining students' general strengths and weaknesses, to assessing a student's reading level, and to assisting teachers, researchers, and others in determining the effects of an intervention on reading comprehension. For example, comparing a student's scores with those of other same-age or -grade students requires a normative assessment. Seeking information about what a student does while reading requires an individual assessment that includes reading aloud. For more information about reading assessments, see Rathvon (2004).

Teachers should consider numerous factors when choosing a test or assessment procedure:

1. The purpose of the testing (screening, progress monitoring, assessing level of reading, research, or assessing students' competence in comparison to peers)
2. The specific information needed about the student's reading comprehension (types of questions missed, level)
3. The number of students being tested (i.e., an individual, a small group, or a whole class)
4. The length of the test (e.g., shorter tests can be easier to give and less stressful for the student, but may not have enough questions or types of tasks to provide sufficient information about a student's performance)
5. Whether the test is an individually or group-administered test

TABLE 2.2. An Overview of Different Types of Comprehension Assessments

Type	Description
Norm-referenced tests	Published tests administered under standardized conditions (e.g., with computerized answer sheets, timed); students' scores are compared with those of a normative sample.
Criterion-referenced tests	Students' test scores are compared with predetermined criterion levels that indicate mastery of a skill or content; informal reading inventories are a type of criterion-referenced test.
Curriculum-based assessment	Tests are based on the actual curriculum used in the classroom, and students are assessed regularly and their progress monitored.
Curriculum-based measurement	Students are assessed frequently with standard, brief tests; scores are monitored over time to assess progress.
Interviews and questionnaires	Students respond orally or in writing to a list of questions designed to assess their understanding of the reading process and their knowledge of reading strategies.
Observation	Examiners observe students' reading behaviors, using checklists, anecdotal records, or ethnographic note taking.
Retelling	Students are prompted to retell or reconstruct what they remember about what they have just finished reading.
Think-alouds	Students are prompted to voice their thoughts before, during, and after reading.

6. The number of forms available with the test, particularly if multiple administrations are needed (e.g., many norm-referenced tests come with two forms, making them useful for assessing progress over time—students are given one version of the test as a pretest and another as a posttest)
7. For norm-referenced tests, the extent to which the norming sample is similar to the students to whom the test will be administered
8. The examiner's qualifications (e.g., whether the tester has the skills to give highly specific tests)
9. The amount of training needed to administer a test, score it, and interpret results (e.g., norm-referenced tests typically require some training)

Reading comprehension measures should help teachers monitor the comprehension of their students over time and provide information that is useful in designing reading comprehension intervention programs. Teachers can ask themselves (Williams, 2000):

- What tasks are most appropriate for evaluating whether my students really comprehend what they read?
- Do these tasks provide useful information for instructional purposes?

Regardless of the method used, when assessing comprehension it is important that the material students are asked to read is at their instructional level (rather than frustration level) and that they can read the passage with adequate fluency. If the student cannot read at least 95% of the words, comprehension will be hampered (Gunning, 2002). Similarly, if the student is a slow, laborious reader (though accurate), comprehension will suffer.

Norm-Referenced Tests

Traditional norm-referenced tests—such as the Gates–MacGinitie Reading Tests, the Gray Oral Reading Test, the Iowa Test of Basic Skills, the Group Reading Assessment and Diagnostic Evaluation (GRADE), or the Stanford Achievement Test—provide an overall measure of reading comprehension and an indicator of how a student compares with age-level and grade-level peers (i.e., the normative sample). On these measures students typically read brief narrative and expository passages and are asked to answer comprehension questions about each passage. Questions about narrative passages generally focus on the setting, characters, sequence, and plot of a story. Questions about expository text typically ask about the main idea and supporting details. Although some questions require inferential thinking, most rely on straight recall. The extent to which readers are able to identify this predetermined information determines at what point they are placed on a continuum ranging from novice to expert reader (Bintz, 2000). Most norm-referenced tests can be used with large groups and have the advantage of being relatively easy to administer and score (see Table 2.3).

TABLE 2.3. A Sample of Norm-Referenced Reading Tests

Title	Ages	Estimated testing time	Key elements of assessment	Validity and reliability	Administration
Aprenda: La Prueba de Logros en Español—3rd Edition (Harcourt Assessment, 2004)	K–12	60–80 minutes (for entire test, less for comprehension subtest only)	Riddles, modified Cloze tests, and comprehension questions. Test also contains listening comprehension and English as a second language assessment sections.	Data not available	Individual
Batería III Woodcock–Muñoz: Pruebas de Aprovechamiento (Riverside, 2005)	Pre-K–grade 12	Varies	Passage comprehension (a cloze task)	*Reliability:* .80 or higher, based on cluster interpretation; no other reliability information specified. *Validity:* Publisher reports good validity based on a large and representative norming sample ($N = 8,818$) and co-norming of two batteries.	Individual
Gates–MacGinitie Reading Tests (MacGinitie, MacGinitie, Maria, & Dreyer, 2000)	Grades K–12 and adult reading	55–75 minutes	Word meanings (levels 1 and 2); comprehension (levels 1 and 2: short passages of one to three sentences; levels 3 and up: paragraph reading)	*Reliability:* Internal consistency by subscale for each level for both fall and spring administrations range from upper .80s to .90s for grades 1–12. *Validity:* Data are provided largely by demonstrating the significant relationships between the Gates–MacGinitie and other measures of reading vocabulary and comprehension.	Group
Gray Oral Reading Test—Diagnostic (Bryant & Wiederholt, 1991)	5 years, 6 months–12 years, 11 months	40–90 minutes	Paragraph reading with five multiple-choice questions; *word identification; morphemic analysis; contextual analysis; word ordering*	*Reliability:* All average internal consistency reliabilities are above .94; test–retest and alternative-form reliability are very high (above .90). *Validity:* Established by relating the Gray Diagnostic Reading Test to other measures.	Individual
Gray Oral Reading Test-4 (Wiederholt & Bryant, 2001)	6 years–18 years, 11 months	15–45 minutes	Fourteen separate stories, each followed by five multiple-choice comprehension questions	*Reliability:* Internal coefficients are above .90; test–retest and alternative-form reliabilities are very high (above .90). *Validity:* Established by relating the Gray Oral Reading Test to other measures.	Individual

(continued)

TABLE 2.3. (continued)

Title	Ages	Estimated testing time	Key elements of assessment	Validity and reliability	Administration
Gray Silent Reading Test (Wiederholt & Blalock, 2000)	7 years–25 years, 11 months	15–30 minutes	Thirteen passages with five comprehension questions each	*Reliability:* Coefficients are at or above .97; test–retest and alternative-form reliability are very high (above .85). *Validity:* Established by relating the Gray Silent Reading Test to other measures, including the Gray Oral Reading Tests.	Individual, small group, or entire class
Group Reading Assessment and Diagnostic Evaluation (GRADE; Williams, 2001)	Pre-K and up	45 minutes to 2 hours (depending on level and how many subtests used)	Sentence comprehension (a clcze task) and passage comprehension (student reads a passage and responds to multiple-choice comprehension questions). Also assesses listening comprehension.	*Reliability:* Coefficients for alternate form and test–retest in the .90 range. *Concurrent and predictive validity:* Assessed using a variety of other standardized reading assessments.	Individual or group
Iowa Test of Basic Skills (ITBS; Hoover, Hieronymus, Frisbie, & Dunbar, 1996)	K and up	43 minutes for reading subtest	Reading comprehension is assessed with comprehension questions that evaluate critical thinking and interpretation	*Reliability:* 84 coefficients (internal consistency) reported for the various subtests; six are in the .70s; others are in the .80s and .90s. The composite score reliabilities are all .98. *Validity:* Established through research studies; no other data reported.	Individual or group
Kaufman Test of Educational Achievement—Revised—Normative Update (K-TEA-R/NU; Kaufman & Kaufman, 1998)	Grade 1 and up	30–60 minutes	Reading comprehension is assessed by asking students to follow written instructions	*Reliability:* Overall reliability coefficients ranged from .87 to .95 for all ages. *Validity:* Data that correlate performance on both forms of the K-TEA with other achievement tests are presented in the manual (e.g., K-ABC ranged from .83 to .88; PIAT ranged from .75 to .86).	Individual or group
Stanford 10 Reading Test (Harcourt Assessment, 2002)	Grades K–12	1 hour	Reading comprehension is assessed with narrative passages followed by open-ended questions focusing on three levels of comprehension (initial understanding, relationships in text and real-life, and critical analysis)	*Reliability:* Assessed using internal consistency measures, alternate-form measures, and with repeated-measurement. *Validity:* Determined using other standardized assessments (e.g., SAT-9, Otis-Lennon). This assessment was standardized using a nationwide representative sample of students in 2002.	Individual

Test	Ages/Grades	Time	Content	Specific information is provided in the test manual.	Administration
Test of Early Reading Ability–3 (Reid, Hresko, & Hammill, 2001)	Grades pre-K–2	20 minutes	Comprehension of words, sentences, and paragraphs (also tests relational vocabulary, sentence construction, and paraphrasing)	*Reliability:* High across all three types of reliability studied. All but 2 of the 32 coefficients reported approach or exceed .90; coefficients were computed for subgroups of the normative sample (e.g., African Americans, Latinos) as well as for the entire normative sample. *Validity:* New validity studies have been conducted; special attention has been devoted to showing that the test is valid for a wide variety of subgroups as well as for a general population.	Individual
Test of Reading Comprehension (Brown, Hamill, & Wiederholt, 1995)	7 years–17 years, 11 months	30–90 minutes	Syntactic similarities (students asked to select two sentences conveying the same meaning); paragraph reading (six paragraphs with five questions each). Sentence sequencing (five randomly ordered sentences for the student to put in the correct order); reading the directions of schoolwork	*Reliability:* .90 range. *Validity:* Criterion validity measures assessed using a variety of measures across several examinations (summarized in the examiner's manual).	Individual, small group, or entire class
Woodcock Reading Mastery Test (WRMT) (Woodcock, 1998)	5 years–75+	10–30 minutes	Word comprehension (antonyms, synonyms, analogies); passage comprehension	*Reliability:* Internal consistency split half reliability: .94–.99 No alternate-form, test-retest or interrater reliability information presented. *Validity* (content): Classical item selection procedures and Rasch-model procedures; some item selection based on correlation with 1977 Woodcock Johnson; content validity of Letter Identification subtest has been questioned. Criterion-related: moderate to high correlation coefficients between WRMT-R and 1977 WJ Reading Tests. *Construct:* Test and cluster intercorrelations between .62 and .96.	Individual

Limitations

Norm-referenced tests have been criticized for being too focused on lower-level comprehension processes and unlike real-life reading tasks. Questions are typically presented in a multiple-choice format, so guessing becomes a factor. Also, standardized tests do not adequately account for the effects of socioeconomic and cultural-linguistic differences on student performance (Snyder, Caccamise, & Wise, 2005). Often a test has not been normed with a population that includes a sufficient number of English-language learners, for example, or students living in high poverty areas. Efforts in recent years have focused on trying to improve standardized tests. The National Assessment of Education Progress (NAEP), the Stanford Achievement Tests–9 (SAT-9), and numerous statewide assessments have steadily shifted from objective multiple-choice questions to questions that require more open-ended responses (Sarroub & Pearson, 1998). The intent is to better assess students' ability to *think* about a passage and to require them to explain their thinking.

However, Bintz (2000) argues that these changes do not go far enough. He remains concerned that reading comprehension tests focus too much on the reader's ability to understand and recall the author's intended meaning of text. These criteria, he contends, are constraining because they focus on what readers *should* be comprehending rather than what and how they *are* comprehending. He notes that it is how the reader interacts with the text that ultimately affects understanding, and traditional assessment methods stop short of assessing this aspect of the reading process. Reading comprehension *starts* (rather than ends) with an understanding of what the author intends to convey. To accurately determine what a reader comprehends, it is important to access the thinking processes that continue after this initial understanding takes place. These processes include forming perspectives, extending, analyzing, questioning, taking a stance, shifting interpretations, rethinking about the self as a reader, reflecting, and thinking critically (e.g., about disconnects and anomalies). Bintz suggests using alternative procedures to tap into these key processes.

Criterion-Referenced Tests

Criterion-referenced tests (CRTs) assess the extent to which students have mastered a skill based on a preestablished criterion. Unlike norm-referenced tests that compare a student's performance to that of other students, CRTs determine how well a student is making progress toward mastery of specific skills or subject matter. There are many available commercial CRTs that assess reading comprehension (see Table 2.4), or teachers can design their own. These assessment tools are constructed in relation to scope and sequence charts in a particular subject area, so that the skills they evaluate progress from the easiest to the most difficult. Because of this structure, CRTs are ideally suited for the purposes of (1) determining the goals and objectives for students' Individualized Educational Plans (IEPs), and (2) evaluating students' progress toward achieving those goals. They are typically given as

TABLE 2.4. A Sample of Criterion-Referenced Assessments

Title	Ages	Estimated testing time	Key elements of comprehension assessment	Administration
Analytical Reading Inventory—6th Edition (Woods & Moe, 1999)	Grade K and higher	Unknown	Student reads leveled narrative and expository passages (aloud and silently), retells passages, and answers specific comprehension questions. Listening comprehension can also be assessed.	Individual
Bader Reading and Language Inventory–3 (Bader, 1998)	Pre-K and higher	Varies depending on subtests given	Graded reading passages used to asses silent reading comprehension (also listening comprehension).	Individual
Basic Reading Inventory—7th Edition (Johns, 1997)	Pre-K and higher	Varies depending on subtests given	Oral and silent reading comprehension assessed through retelling and comprehension questions. English and Spanish	Individual
Developmental Reading Assessment (Beaver, 1997)	Grades K–3	About 20 minutes	Comprehension is assessed through story retelling and comprehension questions with graded reading passages.	Individual
KeyLinks (Harcourt, Brace Educational Measurement, 1996)	Grade 1 and higher	Varies	Reading comprehension of three genres (narrative, informational, and functional text) assessed with open-ended and multiple-choice questions.	Individual and group
Flynt–Cooter Reading Inventory for the Classroom (Flynt & Cooter, 1998)	Grade 1 and higher	15–30 minutes	Student reads a leveled passage of text silently and then retells what was read. Listening comprehension can also be assessed.	Individual
Qualitative Reading Inventory, 4th Edition (QRI; Leslie & Caldwell, 2005)	Emergent to high school	30–40 minutes	Comprehension of oral and silent reading measured through story retelling and comprehension questions. Includes a prior-knowledge test. Listening comprehension can also be assessed.	Individual
Riverside Performance Assessment Series (Riverside Publishing, 1994)	Grade 1 and higher	50–120 minutes, depending on level	Reading comprehension assessed through sequencing elements of the story and writing answers to open-ended questions. Available in English and Spanish.	Individual and group
Standardized Reading Inventory–2 (Newcomer, 1999)	6 years–14 years, 6 months	30–90 minutes	Assesses understanding of vocabulary in context and passage comprehension.	Individual

benchmarks to evaluate progress (e.g., once each grading period, but not more often than that). Other assessment approaches are more closely tied to the curriculum and thus are preferable for day-to-day monitoring of progress and instructional decision making (e.g., curriculum-based assessment, observations, and think-alouds). Most CRTs are individually administered, though a few can also be group-administered. Informal reading inventories (IRIs) are a type of CRT.

Informal Reading Inventories

IRIs are individually administered tests that yield information about a student's reading level as well as word analysis and comprehension skills. Some also assess background knowledge and interests. The test administrator keeps a running record while the student reads different passages aloud, and then asks comprehension questions. Though IRIs were originally developed by teachers, now many commercially produced IRIs are available. IRIs are time consuming to administer, but they do provide in-depth information about a student's literacy skills.

To what extent do IRIs provide useful information about students' reading comprehension? Applegate et al. (2002) recently conducted research on the potential of IRIs to measure students' comprehension processing. They examined the types of open-ended questions and the levels of thinking required in commercial IRIs and found that more than 91% of all questions required only pure recall or low-level inferences rather than higher-level thinking. They concluded that IRIs (1) are overwhelmingly text based, (2) emphasize readers' ability to reproduce ideas rather than integrate and reconstruct them with their own knowledge, and (3) may not be the best tools for assessing higher-level thinking skills. They noted that open-ended questions have the potential to provide much more information about a student's comprehension processes than multiple-choice questions, and they suggest that comprehension measures need to do a better job of distinguishing between readers "who can remember text and those who can think about it" (Applegate et al., 2002, p. 178). They recommend that teachers select IRIs that include more items designed to assess higher-level thinking and encourage publishers to develop IRIs with more of these questions.

Similarly, Dewitz and Dewitz (2003) administered the Qualitative Reading Inventory–3 (QRI-3) as a diagnostic tool for determining students' relative comprehension strengths and weaknesses. They did this by deviating from the guidelines provided by the QRI-3 in order to take a closer look at students' responses to questions. They categorized students' responses and tried to determine why students answered as they did. They noted how students answered questions, what information they drew upon, and the types of inferences they were able to make. Dewitz and Dewitz concluded that "we can improve our understanding of students' comprehension difficulties using available tools like the QRI-3 or other informal reading inventories [by going deeper] into the thinking, or lack thereof, underlying the difficulties that students have in reading comprehension" (p. 434).

They recommended that teachers use IRIs in this way to gather information they can then use to tailor instruction to meet students' needs. One way to do this would be to combine IRIs with think-alouds (described later in this chapter).

Curriculum-Based Assessment

The primary purpose of curriculum-based assessment (CBA) is to systematically assess students' progress toward instructional goals and objectives. Overton (2003) describes CBA as "the very best measure of how much a student has mastered in the curriculum" (p. 299). CBA procedures are based on three fundamental principles: Test items must be taken from the curriculum; evaluations are repeated frequently over time; and results are used to develop instructional plans (King-Sears, 1994).

CBA procedures provide a way to monitor the effectiveness of reading comprehension instructional interventions and to identify learning problems. By using actual reading passages from the curriculum, with accompanying comprehension questions, students' ability to answer questions correctly can be assessed at regular intervals. This assessment information should be recorded on graphs, providing students and teachers with a visual representation of students' progress. By looking at these graphs, teachers can quickly see which students are not improving. Whereas the trend lines of most students slant upward, the lines of students who are struggling remain relatively flat. Klingner and Vaughn (1996) successfully used this procedure to assess the effectiveness of their reading comprehension strategy intervention with English language learners with learning disabilities. Similarly, Ortiz and Wilkinson (1991) recommended CBA as a way to assess the performance of students who are English language learners, in both English and their native language, and determine if they may have learning disabilities. Various forms of CBA have evolved over the years. One of these is curriculum-based measurement (CBM).

Curriculum-Based Measurement

CBM is a type of CBA that includes a set of standard, simple, short-duration fluency measures of basic skills in reading as well as in other subject areas (Deno, 1992; Fuchs & Deno, 1992; Marston & Magnusson, 1985). To implement CBM, assessments of equivalent difficulty are repeated at regular intervals (e.g., weekly or monthly) over a long period of time. In general, assessments are somewhat broad in scope, touching on the variety of skills that are needed to attain curriculum goals (Fuchs & Fuchs, 1999). However, the assessments should also be sensitive enough to pick up change over relatively short periods of time. Student progress is plotted on equal-interval graphs (i.e., a linear graph in which the distance between lines is the same), either manually or with a computerized version of CBM, and displayed in individual and class profiles (Fuchs, Fuchs, Hamlett,

Philips, & Bentz, 1994). This visual representation of the data is easy to interpret and facilitates communication among teachers, parents, students, and others (Deno, 1992). One CBM procedure, in particular, has been validated for assessing reading fluency and comprehension (Shinn & Bamonto, 1998). Students complete a maze reading activity (i.e., multiple-choice cloze task), and the scorer keeps track of the number of correct word choices.

Although CBA and CBM procedures provide a quick indication of students' reading comprehension levels and are useful for monitoring their progress, they do not provide an in-depth picture of students' underlying strategic processing. They tell us only what students comprehend at a basic level, not why they make errors. Like traditional measures, CBA and CBM have been criticized for providing only a narrow portrayal of students' comprehension. Yet, when implemented in combination with other procedures, they can be a valuable tool.

How to Use CBM. Following is an example of how you might use CBM to track students' progress in reading fluency and comprehension, using a maze fluency measure (Fuchs & Fuchs, 2003):

- First, obtain or create the maze fluency passages that represent alternate forms of the difficulty level expected at the end of the year. To generate a maze task, delete every seventh word in a passage and replace it with three multiple-choice responses. Do this for several passages of the same difficulty level.
- Once each week (or month), present each student with a maze passage for 2.5 minutes and record the number of correct responses.
- Record each student's scores over time on a graph. To see how students are progressing, set up a graph with the correct response items on the *y* axis and the weeks/months of instruction or evaluation dates on the *x* axis. Determine a performance goal. The information used to set a goal might come from a CBM assessment, be based on an individual goal, or be based on grade-level expectations. To monitor progress using this information, create a goal line by drawing a line between the first score, or baseline score, and the predicted outcome score. Figure 2.1 presents a maze fluency CBM graph for "Tanya" for 1 school year. Evaluate each student's scores to monitor his or her progress and make instructional adjustments. If scores fall below the goal line, the student is not progressing as expected. If a score falls on or above the goal line, a student is making adequate progress. Share this information with students so that they can see their progress and generate goals for themselves.
- Use the results of the CBM to make instructional decisions based on student progress.
- Many CBM measures provide estimates of typical progress (slopes) so teachers can judge if students are on track for meeting end-of-year goals. If a student's slope is increasing, he or she is making progress toward the annual goal; if the slope decreases or is flat, the student is not benefiting from instruction. In this case,

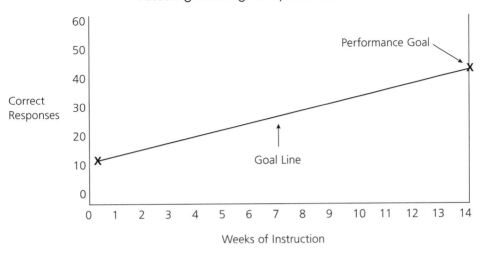

FIGURE 2.1. Maze fluency CBM graph for Tanya.

the teacher should make changes or provide additional instruction. For example, if a student has 3 points that lie above the goal line, you can raise the end-of-year goal and move the goal line upward (a steeper line indicates faster progress). If a student has 2–3 points in a row that are below the goal line, progress is less than expected and instruction should be adjusted to increase learning (Wright, 2006). Teachers can also learn about instruction by comparing progress among students in a class or grade. If most of the students in the class fail to make progress, the instructional program may need to be enhanced. If only a few students make little or no progress, an effective instructional response would be to intensify and specialize instruction for those students.

Interviews and Questionnaires

Interviews and questionnaires are informal assessment measures designed to elicit students' understanding of the reading process and their knowledge of reading strategies (Garner, 1992). These assessment tools provide useful information for the teacher and can also promote students' self-awareness of the underlying processes involved in reading. Oral interviews are conducted individually or in small groups, whereas written questionnaires can be group-administered. Unlike the prompted think-aloud procedure (described in a subsequent section), interviews and questionnaires usually are not linked with a specific reading passage.

How to Use Interviews

Interviews can be informal or more structured. In Figure 2.2 we provide a list of possible interview questions and follow-up probes (adapted from Gunning, 2002). Gunning suggests that questions should not be asked all in one sitting but

What do you do before you start reading?
- Do you read the title and headings?
- Do you look at the pictures?
- Do you predict what the passage might be about?
- Do you ask yourself what you already know about the topic?

What do you do while you're reading?
- Do you think about what you're reading?
- Do you stop sometimes and ask yourself what you've read about so far?
- Do you picture in your mind the people, places, and events you're reading about?
- Do you imagine that you're talking with the author while you're reading?

What do you do when you come to a word you don't understand?
- Do you look for clues and try to figure it out?
- Do you use a glossary or dictionary?

When you come to a part of the text that is confusing, what do you do?
- Do you read it again?
- Do you just keep reading?
- Do you try to get help from pictures or drawings?

After you finish reading, what do you do?
- Do you think about what you've read?
- Do you do something with the information you've learned?
- Do you compare what you've just read with what you already knew?

FIGURE 2.2. Strategy interview. Adapted from Gunning (2002). Copyright 2002 by Prentice Hall. Adapted by permission.

rather used flexibly and interspersed a few at a time in pre- and postreading discussions.

Questionnaires

Questionnaires provide a similar means of learning about students' strategic processing. Because responses are written, the test can be group-administered. Thus, they potentially provide a time-saving way to collect data. Mokhtari and Reichard (2002) developed the Metacognitive Awareness of Reading Strategies Inventory (MARSI), a self-report instrument, to assess adolescent and adult readers' metacognitive awareness and their perceptions about their use of strategies while reading academic texts (see Figure 2.3). Like other written questionnaires, the MARSI can be administered individually or in groups. It is relatively brief, and is intended to supplement other comprehension measures rather than serve as a comprehensive or stand-alone tool. It provides teachers with a feasible way to monitor the type and number of reading strategies students implement. In addition, it helps students become more aware of the reading strategies they use. However, as with other self-report measures, it can be difficult to know for certain if students are actually engaging in the strategies they report using.

Directions: Listed below are statements about what people do when they read *academic or school-related materials* such as textbooks or library books.

Five numbers follow each statement (1, 2, 3, 4, 5), and each number means the following:

- **1** means "I **never or almost never** do this."
- **2** means "I do this **only occasionally**."
- **3** means "I **sometimes** do this" (about **50%** of the time).
- **4** means "I **usually** do this."
- **5** means "I **always or almost always** do this."

After reading each statement, **circle the number** (1, 2, 3, 4, or 5) that best applies to you. Please remember that there are **no right or wrong answers** to the statements in this inventory.

Strategy (and Type)	Scale
1. I have a purpose in mind when I read (G).	1 2 3 4 5
2. I take notes while reading to help me understand what I read (S).	1 2 3 4 5
3. I think about what I know to help me understand what I read (G).	1 2 3 4 5
4. I preview the text to see what it's about before reading it (G).	1 2 3 4 5
5. When text is difficult, I read aloud to help me understand what I read (S).	1 2 3 4 5
6. I summarize what I read to reflect on important information in the text (S).	1 2 3 4 5
7. I think about whether the content of the text fits my reading purpose (G).	1 2 3 4 5
8. I read slowly but carefully to be sure I understand what I'm reading (P).	1 2 3 4 5
9. I discuss what I read with others to check my understanding (S).	1 2 3 4 5
10. I skim the text first and note features like length and organization (G).	1 2 3 4 5
11. I try to get back on track when I lose concentration (P).	1 2 3 4 5
12. I underline or circle information in the text to help me remember it (S).	1 2 3 4 5
13. I adjust my reading speed according to what I'm reading (P).	1 2 3 4 5
14. I decide what to read closely and what to ignore (G).	1 2 3 4 5
15. I use dictionaries or glossaries to help me understand what I read (S).	1 2 3 4 5
16. When text becomes difficult, I pay closer attention to what I'm reading (P).	1 2 3 4 5
17. I use tables, figures, and pictures in text to increase my understanding (G).	1 2 3 4 5
18. I stop from time to time and think about what I'm reading (P).	1 2 3 4 5
19. I use context clues to help me better understand what I'm reading (G).	1 2 3 4 5
20. I restate ideas in my own words to better understand what I read (S).	1 2 3 4 5
21. I try to picture or visualize information to help remember what I read (P).	1 2 3 4 5
22. I use aids like boldface and italics to identify key information (G).	1 2 3 4 5
23. I critically analyze and evaluate the information presented in the text (G).	1 2 3 4 5
24. I go back and forth in the text to find relationships among ideas in it (S).	1 2 3 4 5
25. I check my understanding when I come across conflicting information (G).	1 2 3 4 5
26. I try to guess what the material is about when I read (G).	1 2 3 4 5
27. When text becomes difficult, I reread to increase my understanding (P).	1 2 3 4 5
28. I ask myself questions to see if I understood what I read (S).	1 2 3 4 5
29. I check to see if my guesses about the text are right or wrong (G).	1 2 3 4 5
30. I try to guess the meaning of unknown words or phrases (P).	1 2 3 4 5

(continued)

FIGURE 2.3. Metacognitive Awareness of Reading Strategies Inventory. Adapted from Mokhtari and Reichard (2002). Copyright 2002 by The American Psychological Association. Adapted by permission.

Scoring Rubric for *Metacognitive Awareness of Reading Strategies Inventory*

Student name: _____ Age: ____ Grade in school: _____ Date: _____

1. Write your response to each statement (i.e., 1, 2, 3, 4, or 5) in each of the blanks.
2. Add up the scores under each column. Place the result on the line under each column.
3. Divide the subscale score by the number of statements in each column to get the average for each subscale.
4. Calculate the average for the whole inventory by adding up the subscale scores and dividing by 30.
5. Compare your results to those shown below.
6. Discuss your results with your teacher or tutor.

GLOBAL (G)	PROBLEM-SOLVING (P)	SUPPORT (S)
1. _____	8. _____	2. _____
3. _____	11. _____	5. _____
4. _____	13. _____	6. _____
7. _____	16. _____	9. _____
10. _____	18. _____	12. _____
14. _____	21. _____	15. _____
17. _____	27. _____	20. _____
19. _____	30. _____	24. _____
22. _____		28. _____
23. _____		
25. _____		
26. _____		
29. _____		

GLOB score _____ PROB score _____ SUP score _____ Overall score _____

GLOB mean _____ PROB mean _____ SUP mean _____ Overall mean _____

Key to mean scores: 3.5 or higher = high   2.5–3.4 = medium 2.4 or lower = low

Interpreting your scores: The overall mean indicates how often you use reading strategies when reading academic materials. The mean for each subscale of the inventory shows which group of strategies (i.e., global, problem-solving, and support strategies) you use most when reading. You can tell if you score very high or very low in any of these strategy groups. Note, however, that the best possible use of these strategies depends on your reading ability, the type of material read, and your purpose for reading it. A low score on any of the subscales indicates that there may be some strategies you might want to learn about and consider using when reading.

Global reading strategies include setting purpose for reading, activating prior knowledge, checking whether text content fits purpose, predicting what text is about, confirming predictions, previewing text for content, skimming to note text characteristics, making decisions in relation to what to read closely, using context clues, using text structure, and using other textual features to enhance reading comprehension. (Items 1, 3, 4, 7, 10, 14, 17, 19, 22, 23, 25, 26, 29)

(continued)

FIGURE 2.3. *(continued)*

Problem-solving strategies include reading slowly and carefully, adjusting reading rate, paying close attention to reading, pausing to reflect on reading, rereading, visualizing information read, reading text out loud, and guessing meaning of unknown words. (Items 8, 11, 13, 16, 18, 21, 27, 30)

Support reading strategies include taking notes while reading, paraphrasing text information, revisiting previously read information, asking self questions, using reference materials as aids, underlining text information, discussing reading with others, and writing summaries of reading. (Items 2, 5, 6, 9, 12, 15, 20, 24, 28)

FIGURE 2.3. *(continued)*

Observations

Observations are an integral part of the assessment process and provide evidence of what children actually do rather than just what they *say* they do (Baker, 2002). Observing students while they are engaged in peer tutoring or cooperative learning activities that involve the application of reading comprehension strategies can be particularly illuminating. Listening to how a tutor describes strategy implementation to another student, for example, can provide useful information regarding what the student knows and can do (Klingner & Vaughn, 1996). It is also useful to observe students during independent reading time.

How to Conduct Observations

There are multiple ways of conducting and recording observations. One approach is to use an observation checklist that includes various reading behaviors. The teacher or other observer simply notes which reading-related activities are observed and which are not. We provide two sample checklists. The first is used to examine students' understanding of narrative text (see Figure 2.4). The second checklist is used to evaluate students' performance during independent reading time. Once a semester teachers fill out this form for each student and meet with the student individually to discuss his or her improvement (see Figure 2.5).

Another method is to keep anecdotal records (Gunning, 2002). The observer should record the time, date, setting, and names of those involved, in addition to information about a student's reading behaviors. For example:

> "11:20, 9/23/05: John seems to be doing better at monitoring his understanding and using contextual clues to figure out word meanings. He just asked me for the definition of a key term in his social studies textbook and was able to figure out the word's meaning when I prompted him to reread the sentence looking for clues."

Anecdotal records can be quite brief. We suggest that teachers keep a notepad handy for recording comments about students. Some teachers maintain a spiral notebook and use dividers to create a separate section for each student. Other

Student _____

Teacher _____ Date _____

Directions: Use the following system to record student behavior:

N = Student does not engage in behavior.
B = Student is beginning to engage in behavior.
D = Student is developing the behavior.
P = Student is proficient in the behavior.

Add comments to support your notations.

_____Names characters   _____Describes setting

_____Identifies time/place   _____Identifies problems

_____Identifies solutions   _____Predicts outcomes

_____Identifies mood   _____Describes author's view

_____States theme of story   _____Retells story

Comments:

FIGURE 2.4. Students' understanding of narrative text checklist. Adapted from Pike and Salend (1995). Copyright 1995 by The Council for Exceptional Children. Adapted by permission.

Name _____ Date _____

Rating Scale: A = Almost Always   S = Sometimes   R = Rarely

Chooses Appropriate Books

_____ Chooses easy, just right, and too hard books accurately and with confidence.

Reads Independently

_____ Initiates own reading.

_____ Spends almost all of independent reading time really reading.

Uses Reading Strategies

_____ Rereads to solve problems when comprehension breaks down.

_____ Uses meaning and pictures to help figure out words.

_____ Uses decoding to help figure out words.

_____ Relates reading to own prior experiences.

_____ Makes predictions about what will happen next.

_____ Relates reading to other books and prior knowledge.

_____ Summarizes important points.

_____ Generates questions about content.

Participates in a Community of Readers

_____ Talks about books with classmates.

_____ Raises and explains problems and confusions.

FIGURE 2.5. Reading Behavior Checklist. Adapted from Roller (1996). Copyright 1996 by The International Reading Association. Adapted by permission.

teachers give students their own journals to keep with them during reading activities. With this method the teachers' comments are available to students, and students can add their own reflections. Anecdotal records should be reviewed periodically as a way to keep track of students' areas of need as well as their improvements over time.

Ethnographic note taking is similar to anecdotal record keeping except that notes are more elaborate. Ethnographic note taking is useful when the goal is to focus attention on a specific student (Irwin, 1991). This process involves taking repeated and detailed notes for an extended period of time—or, as Irwin describes, writing "as much as possible as often as possible" (p. 196). Klingner, Sturges, and Harry (2003) provide a detailed explanation of how to use ethnographic observation and note-taking techniques to learn about students' reading practices.

Limitations

A limitation of observations is that it can be difficult to know for certain what comprehension strategies a student is using or why he or she may be behaving in a particular way. We cannot actually observe thought processes, only the outcomes of these processes (e.g., what the child does or says). Therefore, it is important to be cautious when interpreting observation notes and to recognize that there can be alternative explanations for a child's actions. For example, a child who does not volunteer to answer comprehension questions and who seems to remember little might simply be shy or intimidated when speaking in front of others. A child who has difficulty answering questions may have a limited vocabulary or be in the process of acquiring English as a second language (Klingner, 2004). Another limitation of observation methods is that they can be time consuming. However, by combining observations with other assessment methods, the teacher is likely to obtain a more comprehensive picture of students' skills.

Retelling

Oral retelling is a useful technique for monitoring students' reading comprehension. The examiner simply asks the student to retell or reconstruct what was read. Because retelling requires the integration of many skills that are part of the comprehension process, asking students to retell something they have read provides a valuable alternative to traditional questioning techniques for evaluating their reading comprehension. Retelling a story entails understanding, remembering, and sequencing the events and major concepts presented in text (Hansen, 1978). Students must remember factual details and be able to relate them in some organized, meaningful pattern. Additionally, they need to come up with inferences to compensate for information they are not able to recall clearly so that they can reconstruct a coherent retelling.

An advantage to retelling is that the teacher can learn a great deal about what the student understands and where he or she may have gaps. This information is helpful when determining which comprehension skills the student still needs to learn. An interesting research finding is that English language learners have been able to retell more in their native language than in English, even when reading English language text. This finding is noteworthy if the examiner's goal is to determine how much a student understands when reading English text, because the student may provide a more accurate portrayal of his or her comprehension when encouraged to share this information in his or her native language.

A disadvantage to retelling is that it must be conducted individually and is time consuming to administer and score. Another limitation is that students who have difficulties with expressive language may not be able to convey what they understand. Also, as already noted, English language learners may not be able to articulate their understanding in English.

How to Use Retelling

Retelling is a relatively easy assessment to implement. The procedures are as follows:

1. Select an appropriate text for the student to read. The passage should be at the student's instructional or readability level, and can be narrative or expository.
2. Ask the student to read the passage silently, orally, or both silently and orally (a recommended technique with students who are struggling readers).
3. After the student has finished reading, ask him or her to retell the passage. The specific directions for this vary depending upon what type of passage has been read:
   a. With a narrative retelling (Lipson, Mosenthal, & Mekkelsen, 1999), say:
      i. *Pretend I have never heard this story and tell me everything that happened,* or
      ii. *Start at the beginning and tell me the story.*
   b. With informational text (Gunning, 2002), direct the student to
      i. *Tell me as much information as you can remember from the passage you just read,* or
      ii. *Tell me what you learned from the passage.*
4. If the student provides incomplete information, probe or prompt him or her by asking,
   a. *Can you tell me anything more?* or
   b. *Anything else?*

Students with sufficient writing skills can be asked to write their retellings rather than state them orally. Although this is not a suitable option for students who resist writing or lack these skills (e.g., some students with LD), it can work well with confident writers. An advantage of written retellings is that many students can be asked to retell a story at the same time, thus saving time.

How to Score Retells

Evaluating a student's performance on a retell varies depending on whether the student has been asked to retell a narrative passage or an informational text. With a narrative passage, the student should be able to relay the story's plot and describe its characters and setting. With expository text, the student should be able to convey an understanding of the most important information learned and supporting details. With both types of retellings, sequence is important.

While a student is retelling a passage, note the quality and organization of the retelling, whether all essential information is present, and whether there any inaccuracies that indicate faulty or partial comprehension. Also, observe the student's actions before and during reading for clues about his or her affect and whether he or she seems to be applying comprehension strategies. The following questions can serve as a guide.

1. Does the student accurately depict the main ideas of the passage?
2. Are most or all of the key points included?
3. Does the student accurately recount supporting details?
4. Does the student use the same vocabulary as in the original, or simplify or embellish it?
5. In the case of a narrative retelling:
   a. Does the student provide the beginning, middle, and end of the story, and in the correct order?
   b. Does the student describe the characters and setting in the story?
6. Does the student relate information in the text to personal knowledge?
7. Does the student note interrelationships among ideas?
8. Does the student do anything with the text prior to reading (e.g., seem to read the title and subheadings and look at any pictures) or start reading immediately?
9. While reading, does the student look at a glossary or illustrations or seem to reread portions of text?
10. Does the student seem anxious or withdrawn? Or does the student seem confident and comfortable with the task?

Rubrics can be used as a way to tally the quantity and quality of students' responses. The quality of a response might simply be marked as "low," "moderate," or "high." Or a scale of 0–4 or even 0–5 can be used. For example:

0   No response.
1   An inaccurate and incomplete response.

2 Some information is accurate and some is inaccurate; the response is sketchy.

3 Information is generally accurate and complete, but not well developed.

4 Response is complete and accurate.

5 Response is complete and accurate, plus the student points out interrelationships between elements or makes connections to personal knowledge.

Recording sheets can also be used. For a sample recording sheet for a narrative retelling, see Figure 2.6, and for a sample recording sheet for an informational text retelling, see Figure 2.7.

Retelling with Younger Students or Struggling Readers

Paris and Paris (2003) created a version of the retelling procedure for primary-grade students, called the Narrative Comprehension of Picture Books task. Students retell wordless picture books rather than printed text. This procedure has multiple advantages. First, it is useful with young students or struggling readers whether or not they can decode print. Second, it can be used flexibly and adapted to many different narrative picture books. Third, it correlates well with the QRI-2 retelling, suggesting that eliciting retellings from picture narratives is an effective approach. Paris and Paris emphasize the importance of narrative comprehension in beginning reading and contend that narrative competence may be a general feature of children's thinking that is essential for early literacy success as well as cognitive development. They provide convincing evidence that children's understanding of narrative stories is an important foundational skill when learning to read.

Think-Aloud Procedure

With the think-aloud procedure the student is asked to voice his or her thoughts while reading. Asking students to "think aloud" can provide useful insights into their metacognitive and cognitive processing strategies (Irwin, 1991; Kucan & Beck, 1997; Ward & Traweek, 1993), as well as their word learning strategies (Harmon, 2000) and working memory (Whitney & Budd, 1996). It also provides information about the text features students find interesting or important (Wade, Buxton, & Kelly, 1999). These are all processes that have been difficult to evaluate with other assessment procedures. An additional advantage to the think-aloud procedure is that students become more aware of the mental processes they use while reading and can thereby improve their reading comprehension (Oster, 2001).

How to Use the Think-Aloud Procedure

Think-alouds must be administered individually. As with other approaches to comprehension assessment, begin by selecting a passage that is at a student's instructional level. The passage should be readable but not too easy for the student,

Student's Name _____ **Date** _____

Story _____

Story Map (up to 50 points maximum):	**Independent** (full credit)	**Teacher Prompt** (half credit)
SETTING (4 points): Time Period: Location:	(score and comments)	(score and comments)
CHARACTERS (8 points): Main: Other:	(score and comments)	(score and comments)
PROBLEM(S) TO BE SOLVED (8 points):	(score and comments)	(score and comments)
EVENTS (10 points): 1. 2. 3. 4.	(score and comments)	(score and comments)
RESOLUTION (10 points):	(score and comments)	(score and comments)
THEME (10 points):	(score and comments)	(score and comments)

FIGURE 2.6. Sample recording sheet for a narrative retelling. Adapted from Kaiser (1997).

Student's Name _____ **Date** _____

Text _____

Selected by: Student _____ **Teacher** _____

	Unprompted	Prompted
Main Ideas: 2 points: Identifies all main ideas. 1 point: States most of the main ideas. 0 points: Cannot recount any main ideas. Comments:		
Relevant Supporting Details: 2 points: Identifies some details to support each main idea. 1 point: States some details to support some main ideas. 0 points: Does not identify any supporting details. Comments:		
Sequence (states main ideas in order of presentation): 2 points: Correct 1 point: Partial 0 points: Does not indicate recognition of text order. Comments:		
Conclusion 2 points: States conclusion. 1 point: Partially states conclusion. Comments:		
Total Score (8 points possible) **Additional Comments**		

FIGURE 2.7. Sample recording sheet for an informational text retelling. Adapted from Saskatchewan Learning (2002). Copyright 2002 by Saskatchewan Learning. Adapted by permission.

because some cognitive and metacognitive processes are only activated when a text includes challenging components. Then ask the student questions that help him or her think aloud before, during, and after reading, such as the following (adapted from Gunning, 2002):

- *Before reading* (the entire selection): What do you think this passage might be about? Why do you think this?
- *During reading* (after reading each marked-off segment or chunk of text): What were you thinking while you read this section? Were there any parts that were hard to understand? What did you do when you came to parts that were hard to understand? Were there any words that were hard to understand? What did you do when you came across hard words?
- *After reading* (the entire selection): Tell me what the passage was about.

While the student thinks aloud, record his or her responses word for word as closely as possible. Keep in mind that thinking aloud is initially difficult for many students. Therefore, it is important to model this process first and allow students time to practice. Note that the "after reading" prompt is much like that used when asking to students to retell what they have read.

After the student has finished the think-aloud process, analyze his or her responses and note which strategies he or she used, such as:

- Making predictions prior to reading.
- Revising predictions while reading, based on new information.
- Considering (thinking about) information read previously.
- Making inferences.
- Drawing conclusions.
- Making judgments.
- Visualizing or creating mental images.
- Paraphrasing.
- Summarizing.
- Generating questions.
- Reasoning about what was read.
- Monitoring understanding.
- Using context to figure out difficult words.
- Rereading challenging sections.
- Looking at illustrations to aid comprehension.

Finally, draw conclusions about the extent to which the student appears to use strategies effectively and efficiently for monitoring understanding. Use this information to come up with recommendations for instruction.

The think-aloud procedure has been used successfully to detect ineffective processing by students. For example, Monti and Cicchetti (1996) found that struggling readers used few metacognitive and cognitive skills. They tended to (1) focus

more on decoding and pronunciation than comprehension, (2) infrequently activate background knowledge, (3) not monitor their understanding, and (4) raise few
questions about meaning while reading. These are all areas that can improve when
students are taught comprehension strategies (Palincsar & Brown, 1984; Klingner,
Vaughn, Argüelles, Hughes, & Ahwee, 2004). Klingner et al. combined a prompted
think-aloud procedure with follow-up interview questions in an investigation of
reading comprehension strategy instruction with students with LD. The purpose of
the measure was to capture whether and how students applied the comprehension
strategies they had learned on a transfer task (see Appendix 2.1 at the end of this
chapter for a version of this measure).

Limitations

There are several possible limitations to the think-aloud approach, however (Baker,
2002):

1. It may disrupt the process of reading itself
2. It can be difficult for students to carry out, they may not be aware of the
   cognitive processes they are using, and may have trouble articulating what
   they are thinking.
3. Personal characteristics such as age, motivation, anxiety level, and verbal
   ability can affect responses.
4. Students might be cued to provide certain responses by the instructions,
   probes, or questions asked.
5. Finding a passage of just the right level of difficulty can be challenging; students may only reveal the use of cognitive and metacognitive strategies
   when the text is sufficiently difficult, yet passages that are too difficult will
   be too hard for students to read.
6. Think-aloud protocols can be time consuming and difficult to score.

To some extent these limitations can be overcome. For instance, practice with thinking aloud helps students become more aware of, and able to articulate, the mental
processes they are using. Despite its weaknesses, the think-aloud procedure is a
valuable assessment technique. As with other assessment tools we have described,
it is best used in combination with other approaches (Whitney & Budd, 1996).

Assessing Classroom Comprehension Instruction

The final assessment method we discuss in this chapter is not designed to tap students' comprehension processes, but rather to help teachers assess their instruction. Duke and Pearson (2002) provide a valuable list of questions for classroom
teachers (in general or special education) to ask themselves to self-assess their comprehension instruction (see Figure 2.8). Undergoing this process can help teachers

Are students taught to . . .

☐ Identify a purpose for reading?
☐ Preview texts before reading?
☐ Make predictions before and during reading?
☐ Check whether their predictions came true?
☐ Activate relevant background knowledge prior to reading?
☐ Think aloud while reading?
☐ Identify text structure and use it to facilitate comprehension?
☐ Monitor their understanding while reading?
☐ Figure out the meanings of unfamiliar words while reading?
☐ Create visual representations (e.g., story maps) to help with their comprehension and recall?
☐ Determine the most important ideas in what they read?
☐ Summarize what they read?
☐ Generate questions about the important ideas in the text?
☐ Does comprehension strategy instruction include . . .
☐ An explicit description of the strategy and explanation of when it should be used?
☐ Modeling of the strategy?
☐ Guided practice using the strategy, with support as needed?
☐ Opportunities for independent use of the strategy?
☐ Opportunities to apply the strategy in collaboration with others?
☐ Other teaching considerations . . .
☐ Are students taught how to be strategic readers who can use multiple strategies as appropriate (rather than just one at a time)?
☐ Are the texts used for instruction chosen carefully to match students' needs and interests as well as the strategies being taught?
☐ Are student motivation and engagement key concerns while planning and implementing comprehension instruction activities?
☐ Are students' comprehension skills assessed regularly and in multiple ways?

FIGURE 2.8. Checklist for assessing classroom comprehension instruction. Adapted from Duke and Pearson (2002). Copyright 2002 by The International Reading Association. Adapted by permission.

identify the strengths and areas in need of improvement in their comprehension instruction.

CONCLUSION

Perhaps the most important "take-home" message about comprehension assessment is that no one test or procedure should be used alone. It is important for those administering different comprehension measures to be aware of just what each test assesses, what can and cannot be learned, and what the limitations as well as strengths are of each (Klingner, 2004). The best way to assess reading comprehension is with a combination of different measures. Standardized tests, informal reading inventories, interviews and questionnaires, observations, retelling, and think-aloud procedures all have a slightly different purpose and can contribute a unique perspective on students' strengths and areas of need. Through a combination of approaches we can learn much more than whether a student can read a passage and answer comprehension questions correctly, or how the student's comprehension compares with that of others. We can explore the student's underlying thinking processes and uncover information about the strategies he or she uses well, overuses, misuses, or does not use. We can find out how students approach a reading task, how they tap into background knowledge, the information they draw upon to answer questions, whether they answer questions from memory or look back into the text, whether and how they come up with inferences, how they go about trying to determine the meaning of unknown words, and what they do to help themselves remember what they have read. All of this information is helpful when planning instruction.

Comprehension should be assessed frequently as a way to track students' growth and provide useful information that can guide instructional and diagnostic decision making (Klingner, 2004). The assessment tools we have described, when used effectively, can provide psychologists, teachers, and reading specialists with a thorough understanding of the comprehension skills of their students with LD. In addition, they can help struggling readers become more aware of the comprehension processes they are using. We are optimistic that through this increased awareness, students will become more active, strategic, responsive, and thoughtful readers.

APPENDIX 2.1. PROMPTED THINK-ALOUD

Directions:

(Say:) I am going to ask you to read a page from a magazine. While you are reading I'm going to ask you to tell me what you are thinking. You can tell me what you're thinking in either Spanish or English. **(Do:) Ask the student to say what he or she is thinking whenever you come across an asterisk in the text below or whenever the student pauses for 2 seconds or more. You may help the student read words, but do not explain what they mean. Also, after each response, probe for more information by asking, "Anything else?"** Note: The student reads from the actual text, while you use the following:

- **When I give you this to read, what is the first thing you _do_?**

- **Anything else?**

- **What are you thinking about that?** (Note: Here you probe for more information in response to the first question; e.g., if a student says, "I look at the picture," you say, "What are you thinking about when you look at the picture?")

- **Anything else?**

THE PENAN
An Endangered People Living in a Dying Rain Forest

The sun rises, waking the people who live in one of the world's oldest rain forests. Then the people hear the first sounds of the morning. But they don't wake to chirping birds and other natural sounds. They wake to the roar of chainsaws and the thud of falling trees.

- **What are you thinking?**

- **Anything else?**

The people are the Penan. They live in an ancient rainforest on Borneo, an island near Asia. They live by gathering fruits, nuts and roots and by hunting. The Penan way of life, along with the rainforest, is being destroyed. "I just want to cry when I hear the bulldozers and saws," says Juwin Lihan, a Penan leader.

- **What are you thinking?**

- **Anything else?**

A Green Gold Rush
About 25 years ago, logging companies began cutting rainforest trees on Borneo. The loggers call the trees "green gold" because the trees are worth so much money. They cut the trees to make paper, chopsticks, and other products.

From Klingner et al. (2004).

- **What are you thinking?**

- **Anything else?**

As a result of the logging, the land and rivers have become polluted.

- **What are you thinking about that word?**

- **Anything else?**

"Clear rivers have turned into the color of tea with milk," says environment expert Mary Asunta. Government officials, however, say that logging has been good for the area. They point to the more than 100,000 new jobs created in the area by logging companies. The companies have constructed new roads and buildings.

- **What are you thinking?**

- **Anything else?**

Bring Back the Forest
Many of the Penan people don't want the jobs and roads. They want their forest back.
"Before the forest was destroyed, life was easy," says Liman Abon, a Penan leader.
"If we wanted food, there were wild animals. If we wanted money, we'd make baskets. If we were sick, we would pick medicinal plants." Now, he says, that's all gone.

- **What are you thinking?**

- **Anything else?**

- **You may stop reading now. What do you do to help yourself remember what you have read?**

- **Anything else?**

- **What do you do to make sure you understand everything you have read?**

- **Anything else?**

- **What do you do when you do not understand a word or an idea the first time you read it?** (Note: You only need to ask this question if the student does not spontaneously talk about words in response to the previous question.)

- **Anything else?**

Scoring Procedures

The grading of the Prompted Think-Aloud relies on a rubric. Students can earn a total of 6 points on the prereading questions. The areas in which students can earn points include brainstorming what they already know and predicting what they think they will learn. Students also earn points if they mention any strategy from the four following areas: looking at headings or subheadings; looking at words that are italicized, bolded, or underlined; looking at pictures, tables, or graphs; and describing a strategy but not employing it.

For the "during reading" questions, students can earn 2 points for a good "gist" or main idea statement and 1 point for a retelling. Responses to the question asking students to define a word are scored with the following points: no points if the student gives a tangential answer (i.e., answer had nothing to do with the story or the word); 1 point if the student defines the word without making reference to the story; 2 points if the student defines the word while making reference to the story; 1 point if the student's response is a reaction to the word without making reference to the story; and 2 points if the student's response is a reaction to the word while making reference to the story.

Postreading responses are scored on a different scale. Students can earn a maximum of 2 points for each postreading question. They receive 2 points if they mention any one of the following strategies: testing, summarizing, questioning, understanding, or making an outline. They earn only 1 point for the following responses: asking a parent, looking in a dictionary, asking a classmate, or reading it again. All points are added to obtain a single score for each student with the maximum being 26 points.

CHAPTER 3

Vocabulary Instruction

STUDY GROUP PROMPTS

1. Before reading this chapter, ask members of your study group how they are currently enhancing vocabulary knowledge for their students. Make a list of these practices. After reading this chapter, review the list and see if there are vocabulary practices you would change or add.

2. Select a common passage or book that you ask your students to read. Identify the key words that you would teach. Discuss why you would select the words you did. After reading the chapter, consider the words you chose and whether you would make changes.

3. Consider how you might integrate vocabulary instruction throughout the day. After reading the chapter, determine if there are practices you would use to assure that vocabulary instruction is a more highly featured aspect of your program.

4. Identify the ways in which you assess and monitor the vocabulary knowledge of your students. Determine if there are other practices you might want to initiate.

Although it is often missing from instruction, vocabulary is essential to reading comprehension. That is why both the National Reading Panel (National INstitute of Child Health and Human Development, 2000) and the RAND Reading Study Group (2002) investigated vocabulary as an essential part of reading for understanding. Quite simply, it is impossible to understand text if we do not know much about a significant number of the words in the text.

These examples for adults help us understand just how important knowing what words mean is to understanding text. Examine the following passages.

Passage 1

We are acquainted with space–time domains which behave (approximately) in a "Galileian" fashion under suitable choice of reference–body, i.e., domains in which gravitational fields are absent. (Einstein, 1961, p. 77)

Passage 2

Degenerate stars may also be the cause of the so-called planetary nebulae. When these heavy discs of light were first seen in the early telescopes they were mistaken for planets. But they didn't move and had to be outside the solar system. They are gas spheres and the star at the center is blowing off material. The degenerate core is slimming down to the white dwarf stage. Calculations show there is a process of convective dredging going on. (Hawkins, 1983, p. 236)

Chances are that you may not have understood the text in either of the two passages. Why? Terms such as *convective dredging* and *degenerate core* may not be part of your vocabulary. Furthermore, these terms are technical and have specific meanings that are related to physics and astrology and depend on concept and construct knowledge in those fields. For example, most of us would not know what a "white dwarf stage" was, though we would probably conjure up some pretty interesting and inaccurate images. Furthermore, we wouldn't know whether there were stages that preceded and followed the "white dwarf stage" and how those stages related. Overall, vocabulary knowledge and construct knowledge in all text are the essence of comprehension.

HOW DOES TEACHING VOCABULARY
FACILITATE READING COMPREHENSION?

Regardless of what you teach—math, science, history, biology, or government—one of your major responsibilities is to teach key vocabulary and concepts so that students can comprehend what they read and understand the academic language of the discipline. For example, in mathematics, the words *minus, divided,* and *area* have specific meanings that allow students to comprehend math problems. Even if students understand what the words mean generally, they will also need to learn the specific academic meaning of the words. Vocabulary instruction is a necessary part of comprehension instruction because understanding text is significantly influenced by vocabulary development (Baumann & Kame'enui, 1991; Graves, Brunetti, & Slater, 1982; Graves, 1989).

HOW CAN WE ASSESS AND MONITOR VOCABULARY LEARNING?

How do we know that when we work very hard to expose, integrate, teach, and review vocabulary words, students are actually learning them? How do we determine which words students know and understand and which ones slip away? There is probably no area in reading that is more difficult to assess than vocabulary knowledge. Not only is it difficult to assess but typical practices for assessing vocabulary (e.g., write the definition of the word) are often not liked by teachers or students—and actually tell us very little about how well the student knows the word.

More than 40 years ago, Dale (1965) described the stages of knowing the meaning of a word. It may be helpful to consider these stages as we think about assessing how well students know word meaning.

- Stage 1: The student knows nothing about the word—never saw or heard it before.
- Stage 2: The student has heard of the word but has no idea what it means.
- Stage 3: The student knows something about the word when he or she hears or reads it in context.
- Stage 4: The student knows the word well.

Beck and colleagues (Beck, McKeown, & Omanson, 1987) have extended this "word knowing" along a continuum:

- No knowledge of the word
- General sense of the word
- Narrow idea of the word bound by context
- Knowledge of the word but may not be able to recall and use readily
- Rich understanding of the word's meaning and its connection to other words

Teachers may want to consider the following types of questions and instructions as ways of "tapping" student's knowledge about words:

- What does *nomenclature* mean?
- Use *obsequious* in a sentence.
- What is the opposite of *homogeneous*?
- What means the same as *gauche*?
- Give an example of how someone would behave who was *frivolous* with his or her money.

For many students with reading difficulties, these words are either so difficult that they have no idea what they mean, or they have heard of the words but have only a broad idea of their meaning. Simmons and Kame'enui (1998) found that 10-

and 12-year-old students with LD had less extensive vocabularies than peers without disabilities.

There are literally hundreds of thousands of words like these. How can we determine what words students know, what words students are learning, and what words students need to learn? If we are interested in determining whether students are learning the words we are teaching in language arts, social studies, and science, how do we assess them?

ASSESSING VOCABULARY

Whereas assessment and progress monitoring of vocabulary in typical achieving students are exceedingly challenging, the problems are even greater for students with LDs. For many students with reading difficulties, writing and spelling difficulties co-occur, so whenever tests require tapping their knowledge through writing, poor performance may be a result of not knowing the meaning of the word or not being able to write about it. Thus, when constructing progress monitoring measures and using more formal measures, we have to consider what knowledge and skills the measures are tapping.

When oral language is assessed broadly, usually five components are tapped (Rathvon, 2004):

- Phonology—discriminating between and producing speech sounds.
- Semantics—understanding word meaning.
- Morphology—using and understanding word formation patterns that include roots, prefixes, suffixes, and inflected endings.
- Syntax—using correct phrasing and sentence organization.
- Pragmatics—using language to communicate effectively.

For the purpose of teaching vocabulary, we are most interested in determining whether students have knowledge of semantics and morphology. So, what are some ways teachers can determine the progress students are making in acquiring word meaning (semantics) and using word formation patterns (morphology)? Formal assessments of vocabulary (see Figure 3.1) typically ask students to point to pictures that best represent the words provided. Sentence completion measures, in which sentences are read aloud and students select or provide appropriate missing words, are also used. Janet Allen (1999) suggests that we can determine the understanding students have of words by assessing them in meaningful ways.

Using Curriculum-Based Measures to Assess Vocabulary

Some teachers have begun to measure vocabulary and content learning simultaneously by using curriculum-based measurement (CBM). CBM monitors progress by providing regular assessments in a curricular area and tracking students'

ASSESSING INTEGRATION AND MEANINGFUL-USE INSTRUCTION

Single Definition   Inference

Sample 1

A jockey is a   cowboy   You would be most likely   racetrack
                       Wall Street worker to see a working jockey   cow ranch
                       horse racer   at a   sold house
                       furniture mover   post office

Sample 2

Read the following sentence and then answer the question that follows:

   *When the teacher heard that her student had stopped spending time with
   her usual friends, the teacher complimented her for making good choices.*

What do you think the teacher thought of her student's friends?

Sample 3

Four of our words this week were *adolescents, gangs, irresponsible,* and *irrational.*
If I connect those four words by making this statement, "If you take a job where you work with
adolescents, you can count on trouble with gangs, and on irresponsible and irrational behavior,"
I am guilty of doing what?

_____

Sample 4

One of our target words this week was *preposterous.* What kind of in-school behavior would
the principal think was preposterous?

Sample 5

The concept we discussed this week was *prejudice.* How could we use the prefix and the root
word for this word to help us understand its meaning?

Sample 6

The concept we have been studying is *balance.* What might someone do who is trying to find
balance in his or her life?

Sample 7

Four of our target terms this week were *pollution, population control, public transportation,* and
pesticides. In what ways could all of these terms be connected to a larger concept?

FIGURE 3.1. How to assess word understanding in meaningful ways. Reprinted from Allen
(1999). Copyright 1999 by Stenhouse Publishers. Reprinted by permission.

progress over time (Deno, 1985; see Chapter 2 for more information on CBM and
reading comprehension). In a recent study, Espin, Shin, and Busch (2005) used a
CBM vocabulary measure to track middle school students' learning in social
studies. Weekly assessments took about 5 minutes and included 22 words and
definitions generated randomly from a master list of 146 vocabulary terms. Students were asked to match each term with its definition. The authors found that
knowledge of social studies content could be adequately measured by monitor-

ing progress on the vocabulary matching assessment. The use of CBM in this study measured both vocabulary acquisition and social studies content learning, providing further support for the link between vocabulary knowledge and content learning.

Perhaps the first step in assessing vocabulary is to determine what students already know about the essential words in a unit or story. Consider the following steps to determine what students know about words:

1. Review the unit or story. Select the key words that students need to know to understand the story. If there are relatively few key words (three to five), also select difficult words that may not be essential to understanding the story but would enhance students' vocabulary.
2. Consider if there are ways in which the words could be grouped together. Grouping can be based on several types of linkages the words have in common. For example, if the unit is on manufacturing, all of the key words that relate to the production of goods can be grouped together. If the reading is a narrative story, all of the words that describe the characters in the story can be grouped together.
3. Read the words aloud to students and show them the word groupings. Ask them to tell you why the words go together in a group. Support students' responses by extending and linking their ideas with the word meanings and their connection to text.
4. Now ask students to work with a partner and to brainstorm key words or associations that describe or inform the vocabulary words selected.
5. Ask students to share their words and associations. Be sure to clarify if students are providing information that is not related to the word or is misleading.

Most teachers are interested in determining whether students are learning many of the key words they teach. There are many occasions, though, when educators need to know more information about students' vocabularies, and they need to better understand whether their vocabulary problems are small or large. The best way to understand the relative performance of a student's vocabulary is to know how it compares to same-age or same-grade students on a standardized measure of vocabulary.

Are there standardized vocabulary measures? Yes, standardized tests of vocabulary can be administered by teachers that provide information on the relative standing of a student compared to classmates. These measures are often individually administered; however, there are several group-administered vocabulary measures as well. Table 3.1 provides an overview of standardized vocabulary measures, whether they are individually or group-administered, the ages for which they are appropriate, their psychometric characteristics, and how additional information about them can be obtained.

TABLE 3.1. Vocabulary Assessment Instruments

Name	Publisher	Group/age	Administration	Assessment	Psychometrics	Other
The Word Test–2: Elementary and Adolescent	PRO-ED	6 years and up	Individual	Measures expressive vocabulary and other critical semantic features; six subtests.	Reliability–internal consistency: split half .91; no test–retest. Validity: limited information concerning content validity.	Test time: 30 minutes
Adolescent Language Screening Test (ALST)	PRO-ED	11–17 years	Individual	Expressive and receptive vocabulary measured by seven subtests.	Criterion referenced; no data presented on validity and reliability.	Test time: 10–15 minutes
Expressive One-Word Picture Vocabulary Test–2000 Edition (EOWPVT-2000)	PRO-ED	2 years, 0 months–18 years, 11 months	Individual	Measures expressive vocabulary through word–picture associations.	Reliability–internal consistency: alphas .93–.98 (median .96); split-half .96–.99 (median .98); test–retest .88–.97. Interrater reliability high. Validity: strong correlations to other tests, ranging from .67–.90.	Test time: 10–15 minutes
Expressive Vocabulary Test (EVT)	PRO-ED	2 years, 6 months–90+	Individual	Measures expressive vocabulary.	Reliability analysis indicated high degree of internal consistency: split-half reliability .83–.97; alphas range from .90–.98; test–retest .77–.90.	Test time: 15 minutes
Receptive One-Word Picture Vocabulary Test–2000 Edition (ROWPVT-2000)	PRO-ED	2 years, 0 months–18 years, 11 months	Individual	Assesses receptive vocabulary	Reliability–internal consistency: alphas .95–.98 (median .96); split-half .97–.99 (median .98); test–retest .78–.93 (median .84). Interrater very high. Validity: content using item analysis, criterion related closely correlated (.44–.97, median .71) with scores of other vocabulary tests, and construct validity (average correlation .34–.83).	Test time: 10–15 minutes
Comprehensive Receptive and Expressive Vocabulary Test (CREVT-2)	PRO-ED	4 years, 1 months–89 years, 11 months	Individual	Measures both expressive and receptive vocabulary with two subtests.	Reliability: alphas .80–.98 (median .93); alternate forms (immediate) .87–.98 (median .94); test–retest .93–.98 (median .95); alternate forms (delayed) .88–.99 (median .95); interscorer .97–.99 (median .99). Validity: content description using subtest item analysis, conventional item analysis, and differential item functioning analysis, criterion prediction (.39–.92), construct identification.	Test time: 20–20 minutes

52

Test	Publisher	Age/Grade	Administration	Measures	Reliability/Validity	Test time
Receptive–Expressive Emergent Language Test—Third Edition (REEL-3)	PRO-ED	Birth through 3 years	Individual	Measures receptive and expressive vocabulary through two subtests given by caregiver.	Reliability: alphas .95–.98; test-retest .78–.89; interrater (median .99) excellent. Validity: content discription using subtest item analysis, differential item functioning analysis, criterion prediction, construct identity, and subtest interrelationships.	Test time: 20 minutes
Diagnostic Achievement Test for Adolescents-2 (DATA-2)	PRO-ED	Grades 7–12	NA	Measures receptive and expressive vocabulary.	Reliability: alphas 84–98, standard error or measurement (SEM). Validity: content, criterion, and construct.	Test time: 60–120 minutes
Pictorial Test of Intelligence-2 (PTI-2)	PRO-ED	3–8 years	Individual	Measures receptive vocabulary.	Reliability demonstrated using coefficient alpha (.89–.94), test-retest (.57–.91), and interscorer procedures (.95–.98). Validity proven for content description using conventional item analysis, differential item functioning analysis, criterion predition, and construct identification using factor anaylsis subtest item validity.	Test time: 15–30 minutes
Iowa Tests of Educational Development (ITED), Form A	Riverside	Grades 9–12	NA	Measures receptive vocabulary using synonyms.	Reliability: .87–.94. Validity: content, criterion, contruct related.	Test time: < 40 minutes
Iowa Tests of Basic Skills (ITBS), Form A	Riverside	Grade K–8	Group	Measures receptive vocabulary by selecting corresponding pictures or words from a list.	Reliability: KR-20 .85–.98, SEM reliability overall high. Validity: content, construct using intercorrelations and criterion related.	Test time: < 40 minutes
Tests of Achievement and Proficiency (TAP), Forms K, L, and M	Riverside	Grades 9–12	Group	Measures receptive vocabulary using synonyms.	Reliability: KR-20 .85–.95, SEM. Validity: content using subtests, construct inadequate, and criterion.	Test time: 90–275 minutes
Nelson–Denny Reading Test	Riverside	Grades 9–12, college, and adult	Individual	Measures receptive vocabulary, comprehension, and reading rate.	Reliability: Test-retest .89–.95 for vocabulary subtest.	Test time: ~ 35 minutes

(continued)

53

TABLE 3.1. (*continued*)

Name	Publisher	Group/age	Administration	Assessment	Psychometrics	Other
Diagnostic Assessment of Reading with Trial Teaching Strategies (DARTTS)—Using Diagnostic Assessment of Reading (DAR)	Riverside	NA	NA	Measures receptive and expressive vocabulary.	NA	Test time: 20–30 minutes
Group Reading Assessment and Diagnostic Evaluation (GRADE)	AGS	Grades pre-K to adult	Group	Includes vocabulary subtest measures	Reliability: internal .95–.99; alternate form .81–.94; test–retest .77–.98; measures content validity.	Test time: 45–90 minutes
Peabody Picture Vocabulary Test—Third Edition (PPVT-III)	AGS	2 years, 6 months–90+	Individual	Measures receptive vocabulary.	Reliability–internal consistency: alpha .92–.98 (median .95); split-half .86–.97 (median .94); alternate form .88–.96 (median .94); test–retest .91–.94 (median .92). Validity: average correlation of .69 with OWLS Listening Comprehension Scale (internal consistency .84, test–retest .76) and .74 with OWLS Oral Expression Scale (internal consistency .87; test–retest .81). Correlations with measures of verbal ability are .91 (WISC-III), .89 (KAIT), and .81 (K-BIT vocabulary).	Test time: 10–15 minutes
Expressive Vocabulary Test (EVT)	AGS	2 years, 6 months–90+	Individual	Measures expressive vocabulary using one-word responses and picture identification.	Co-normed with PPVT-III. Reliability indicates high degree of internal consistency: split-half .83–.97 (median .91); alphas .90–.98 (median .95); test'retest .77–.90. Median SEM: 4.6. Validity tests include intercorrelations, criterion related, and clinical sample.	Test time: ~ 15 minutes
Woodcock Reading Master Tests—Revised—Normative Update (WRMT-R/NU)	AGS	Grades K–16; 5 years, 0 months–75+	Individual	Measures expressive vocabulary using synonyms and antonyms	Reliability–internal consistency .68–.98 (median .91); split-half clusters median .95 (.87–.98), total median .97 (.86–.99); no test–retest, no interrater. Validity tests included intercorrelations, content, and concurrent.	Test time: 10–30 minutes

54

Test	Publisher	Grade/Age	Administration	Measures	Reliability/Validity	Test time
Johnson Basic Sight Vocabulary Test	Personal Press	Grades 1 and 2	Group	Measures receptive vocabulary using stimulus and distractor words.	No data on reliability or validity.	Test time: 30–45 minutes
Sandler–Futcher Vocabulary Test	Bureau of Educational Measures	Grades 9–13	Group	Measures receptive vocabulary using definition-to-word matching, synonyms, and correct usage.	Reliability: split-half. No other information given. No equivalent-form reliability. Validity: content, no criterion-related.	Test time: 40–45 minutes
Vocabulary Comprehension Scale	Learning Concepts	Grades 2–6	Individual	Measures expressive vocabulary through acting/performing tasks.	No data on reliability available. No validity studies of scale taken.	Test time: 20 minutes
Vocabulary Test for High School Students and College Freshman	Bobbs–Merill	Grades 9–13	Group	Measures receptive vocabulary using word context.	NA	Test time: ~ 15 minutes
Vocabulary Test: McGraw–Hill Basic Skills	McGraw–Hill	Grades 11–14	Group	Measure receptive vocabulary using word meaning and roots and affixes.	NA	Test time: 12 minutes
Word Understanding Test	Hoepfner, Hendricks, & Silverman Monitor	Grades 6–12	Group	Measures receptive vocabulary using a multiple-choice test with synonyms.	Reliability–internal consistency: Interpart correlation .83. Validity: "Should be empirically determined by the user."	Test time: 8–10 minutes
Test of Word Knowledge	Psycho-logical Corporation	5–17 years	Individual	Measures receptive and expressive vocabulary.	Reliability–internal consistency .84–.95; interscorer reliability .90–.99. Validity: content, construct using intercorrelations between subtests, criterion related.	Test time: 31 minutes (level 1); 65 minutes (level 2)
Beery Picture Vocabulary Test and Beery Picture Vocabulary Screening Series	Psycho-logical Assessment Resources	Grades 2–12; 2 years, 6 months–39 years, 11 months	Individual or group	Designed to measure recall of vocabulary.	Reliability–internal consistency: Interscorer .90; test-retest.73–.95; No KR-20. Validity: content, construct, and criterion related.	Test time: 10 minutes per test

WHAT ARE THE BEST PRACTICES
FOR PROMOTING VOCABULARY ACQUISITION?

Whereas teachers may include some sort of vocabulary instruction across subject areas, the challenge is to provide meaningful learning opportunities so that students can go further than only recalling word meanings for a weekly test to develop a deep understanding of words that enables them to apply their understanding across contexts.

Just to keep up with their peers, students need to learn between 2,000 and 4,000 new words per year (Graves, 2004)—that is, approximately 40–50 new words each week! And it takes about 12 encounters with a word to know it well enough to improve reading comprehension (McKeown, Beck, Omanson, & Pople, 1985). "Vocabulary knowledge seems to grow gradually, moving from the first meaningful exposure to a word to a full and flexible knowledge" (Stahl, 2003, p. 19). With this teaching challenge in mind, teachers need to provide a range of experiences with new vocabulary so that students can learn new words in meaningful ways.

Should vocabulary instruction be different for students with disabilities, or are all strategies equally effective? Although many strategies are effective for students with varying abilities, a review of the small body of literature on teaching vocabulary to students with disabilities highlights several strategies (Bryant, Goodwin, Bryant, & Higgins, 2003; Jitendra, Edwards, Sacks, & Jacobson, 2004). Strategies that yielded positive results include:

- Mnemonic or key word strategies that provide phonetic or imagery links to target words.
- Direct instruction of word meanings (e.g., providing definitions, giving synonyms).
- Concept enhancement procedures that assist students in making cognitive connections (e.g., semantic or concept mapping).

In general, regular instruction (several times weekly) was provided for short periods of time, indicating that teachers do not need to devote large portions of instructional time to teaching vocabulary to students with LD. In addition, the most effective strategies included some sort of manipulation of the vocabulary words that encouraged students to actively engage with words and word meanings and provided structured time to practice. Therefore, vocabulary instruction for students with LD should not be limited to one strategy but should combine methods (e.g., direct instruction and mnemonic devices) to maximize word learning (Bryant et al., 2003). Furthermore, as with any instruction, the type of vocabulary strategy should reflect teaching goals (Jitendra et al., 2004). For example, direct instruction methods are most appropriate for introducing new vocabulary, whereas comprehension and generalization are promoted during concept enhancement activities.

Research on vocabulary instruction for students with a range of abilities supports the following components of instruction to promote the acquisition of new words (Graves, 2000). These are described in the following section, with strategies that have been studied with LD populations highlighted throughout.

- Selecting key words to teach.
- Providing definitions that assist in word learning.
- Using mnemonic or key word strategies.
- Making the most of sentence writing.
- Teaching words related to a theme or concept.

Selecting Key Words to Teach

With so many words to learn, one of the first questions teachers ask is how to select which words to teach. Consider an adult with a fully developed vocabulary. Beck and McKeown (1983; Beck, McKeown, & Kucan, 2002) group a person's vocabulary into three tiers. The first tier consists of commonly used and understood words such as *person*, *talk*, and *begin*. These are words that students encounter frequently, so there is usually no need to "teach" them at school. However, even first-tier words will be unknown to some students (e.g., students with disabilities or English language learners). Teachers cannot assume that all students are familiar with tier-one words and should use assessment procedures to verify how to select the types of words that need to be taught directly.

The second tier consists of words that are integral to a mature adult vocabulary because they are used with some frequency across contexts. Stahl and Stahl (2004) refer to these as "Goldilocks" words because they are not too difficult or too easy, but just right. However, these words are used more in written text than in spoken language and are thus likely to be unfamiliar to students. Examples of tier-two words are *prominent*, *conscientious*, *beguile*, and *belligerent*. Tier-two words often need to be addressed through instruction. The third tier contains words that are domain specific with a low frequency in terms of general use. It usually makes sense to learn these words only when they need to be applied in specific contexts. For example, although scientists require a deep and varied understanding of the word *genotype*, for most people it would be appropriate to learn what a genotype is during a science unit on genetics, and the application in that domain would be sufficient.

Once you have selected the key words that students need to know from literature or content-area curriculum, there are many ways to teach them. However, although it may be practical to teach the same words to all students, a review of vocabulary instruction techniques suggests that word lists should be personalized (Blachowicz & Fisher, 2004). Teachers often create a core list of key words to teach and then individualize (by adding additional words or emphasizing fewer words) the list to meet individual student needs. Some of the practices that have been supported by research are discussed below.

Providing Definitions That Assist in Word Learning

The introduction of new words creates interest—and occasionally excitement. The focus of *word introductions* (Beck et al., 2002) is to provide meaningful explanations of a new word with multiple examples that are scaffolded by the teacher, as noted in the following sequence:

1. If applicable, present the word in the context of the story or reading from which the word was selected.
2. Ask students to repeat and write the word.
3. Provide a *student-friendly explanation* of the word by (a) describing it in everyday language that is understandable to your students; (b) using connected language to describe the word in different situations, not single words or short phrases (they lack context and are difficult to remember); and (c) including references to "you," "something," and "someone" to help students make a connection with the new word and their own lives.
4. Ask students to connect what they know by creating their own examples. The teacher asks students to "tell about something you would be *eager* to do." The teacher often has to ask further questions to guide students to come up with an example that is different from the context in the text or that given by the teacher.
5. Students are asked to say and read the word again to establish a link to its phonological representation.

Really knowing and understanding a new word requires frequent and continued exposure by hearing others use it, seeing it in print, and using it yourself. Many students with LD will require ongoing exposure and use of new words to assure that they understand and retain the meaning and use of the words.

Other suggestions that have had positive results include presenting or creating synonyms or antonyms for the key word that are familiar to students. Similarly, providing examples and nonexamples can help enrich understanding, as students try to hone in on a word's meaning in different contexts. One technique is to give students two similar sentences that describe a key word, one that is an example of its definition and one that is not (Beck et al., 2002). In the following illustration, students are presented with an example and a nonexample of the word *encourage*.

Example	*Nonexample*
Before going up to bat, Joey's teammates tell him he's a great player and that he'll get a hit.	Joey's teammates tell him to get a hit this time or else they will lose the game.

If students are using dictionaries or other sources that provide a definition (e.g., sidebars in science or social studies textbooks often provide definitions of key terms), rewriting definitions in their own words can also be helpful. Once they have a working definition of the word, students can then provide examples of it with prompts such as "Tell about a time when you *encouraged* someone"; "What are some things that you could say to *encourage* someone who is feeling frustrated?" The initial activities in which students engage when learning new words are important because they have the potential to peak student's interest (or not) and lay the groundwork for learning the sometimes complex and varied meanings of words.

Using Mnemonic or Key Word Strategies

Mnemonic or key word strategies are memory strategies that assist students in memorizing the definitions of new words. Students with LD benefit from connections created by linking a familiar key word or image with a novel word (Bryant et al., 2003; Jitendra et al., 2004). Although mnemonics can be used for a variety of memory tasks, we highlight a strategy described by Mastropieri and Scruggs (1998) that specifically promotes vocabulary acquisition. In this strategy an association is created between a new word (e.g., *trespass*) and a familiar but unrelated word (e.g., *tiger*). In this case, the teacher created an image of a tiger entering a schoolyard and showed it to the class.

TEACHER: What is the key word for *trespass*?

STUDENT: *Tiger.*

TEACHER: Yes, *tiger* is the key word for *trespass*, and *trespass* means entering a place you are not supposed to enter. Here is a picture of a *tiger trespassing* in a schoolyard. A *tiger* is not supposed to enter a schoolyard. So when you think of the word *trespass*, think of a *tiger* and remember the picture of the *tiger trespassing* in the schoolyard

It is important to note that both teacher-created and student-created mnemonic images are effective for learning the definitions of new words. However, when students create the images, it takes more time and requires careful monitoring and feedback (Mastropieri & Scruggs, 1998).

Making the Most of Sentence Writing

Teachers frequently ask students to write a sentence using a newly learned word. Make the most of these sentences by engaging students actively in the sentences they have written. When students interact with and manipulate new words, their understanding and retention increase (e.g., Blachowicz & Fisher, 2004; Bryant et al., 2003).

• Discuss the various sentences students create using key words by comparing the meaning in different sentences and the types of sentences that are the most useful for word learning. Students can then select which sentence helps them remember the word and can record that example sentence in their notes. Take the word *ripe*, for example. As you can see from the list of sentences below, sentences 1, 2, and 3 include varying meanings of *ripe*, whereas the fourth sentence is not acceptable because it does not provide enough information to glean the meaning of the word.

1. If you pick the banana from the tree before it is ripe, it will be green and taste terrible.
2. The old woman lived to the ripe age of 95.
3. After studying all week, the students were ripe to take the math test.
4. The peach is ripe.

- Another variation on sentence writing is to have students use more than one new word in a sentence. In this way, students can connect new words with each other and challenge themselves to use them accurately in a similar context. Students also enjoy creating stories around a group of key words and then sharing how the same words can result in such different stories.
- Have students create fill-in-the-blank activities with new words. Students can create five sentences with five new words and then have peers "do" their activity. If definitions are not clear, students work together to create sentences that provide a better explanation. Giving feedback about correct usage and acceptable sentences that facilitate understanding is part of the process during any sentence or story-writing activity.

Teaching Students to Monitor Their Understanding of Difficult Words as They Read

Students may fail to recognize that they do not understand certain words or concepts as they read. Students can learn to identify difficult words, sometimes called "clunks," as they read and then use "fix-up" strategies to repair their understanding (Klingner et al., 2001). Fix-up strategies cue students to use word-level skills (e.g., break the word apart and look for smaller words you know) or context clues (e.g., read the sentence without the clunk and see what word makes sense) to assist them in figuring out the meanings of words during reading. Students use fix-up strategies to gain enough information to repair understanding while reading. However, to assist students in gaining a deeper knowledge of important words, teachers must provide additional instruction and practice opportunities. To learn more about using fix-up strategies, see the lesson plans at the end of this chapter and the section on collaborative strategic reading in Chapter 6.

Teaching New Words around a Theme or Concept

Creating concept representations of word meanings assists students in making connections between new words, their existing knowledge, and the concepts being taught in school (Stahl, 1999). For students with LD, using these concept enhancement strategies is more effective for learning new words and remembering them in the future than is using direct instruction alone or other more traditional strategies such as finding dictionary definitions (Jitendra et al., 2004). Among the many instructional practices used to create conceptual representations of new words, we present clarifying tables, semantic maps, concept maps, and Venn diagrams

- Clarifying tables (Ellis & Farmer, 2005) help students organize information about important vocabulary and keep track of the words they have learned (e.g., in a notebook of important words). Teachers may present a word that will be read in literature or content-area text and then complete the clarifying table with students after the word has been encountered. In the following example, the word *mockery* was integral to understanding the character of Mrs. May in *The Borrowers Afloat* by Mary Norton, a book selected by students in a classroom book club. Figure 3.2 is an example of the clarifying table created by the fourth-grade students and their teacher to help them learn and remember the meaning of *mockery*.

- Semantic maps are used to help students learn important words and to make connections with related key words or ideas. Semantic maps are often created as webs with linkages designated by connecting lines. The teacher may lead a semantic mapping activity prior to reading to introduce key terms, activate prior knowledge, and as a preassessment. Alternatively, semantic maps may also be used after reading to summarize and review key terms and ideas and to informally assess student understanding. Figure 3.3 shows a semantic map created after reading a chapter on Egypt. Semantic maps represent many key terms and ideas and allow students to see how the ideas are related to one another.

- If the instructional goal is to define or clarify the meaning of a key concept, teachers may elect to use a concept map. Similar to clarifying tables or semantic maps, concept maps are visual representations of the relationship between the terms associated with a particular concept (e.g., body parts, oceans, migration). Concepts are developed using group discussion to encourage students to share individual expertise (Stahl, 1999). For example, in developing the concept of *sea-*

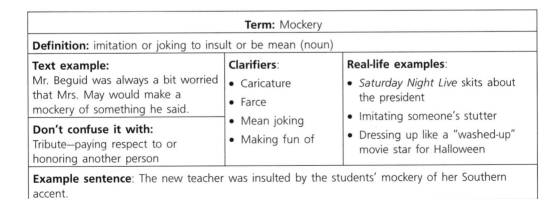

Term: Mockery		
Definition: imitation or joking to insult or be mean (noun)		
Text example: Mr. Beguid was always a bit worried that Mrs. May would make a mockery of something he said.	Clarifiers: • Caricature • Farce • Mean joking • Making fun of	Real-life examples: • *Saturday Night Live* skits about the president • Imitating someone's stutter • Dressing up like a "washed-up" movie star for Halloween
Don't confuse it with: Tribute—paying respect to or honoring another person		
Example sentence: The new teacher was insulted by the students' mockery of her Southern accent.		

FIGURE 3.2. Clarifying table. Reprinted from Vaughn, Bos, and Schumm (2007). Copyright 2007 by Pearson Education. Reprinted by permission.

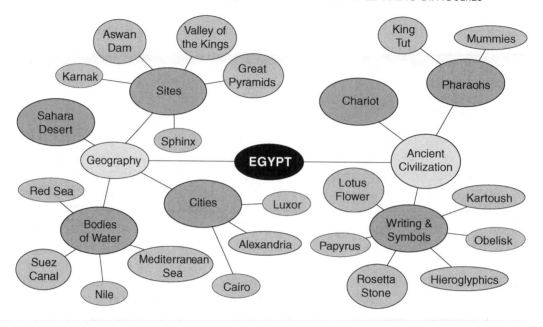

FIGURE 3.3. Example of a semantic map.

sons, one student may have knowledge of the seasons (fall, winter, spring, summer), whereas another student may understand a bit about the earth's rotation around the sun. The process of establishing associations between related vocabulary terms is particularly useful for students with a limited vocabulary or understanding of the concept; these students need assistance to make connections and deepen their understanding. There are many ways to create concept maps. In one study, a teacher and her students created a concept map around the concept of racism (Scott & Nagy, 2004). The grouped discussed racism and the ways to visually represent it. The teacher also added key terms that were essential for students to learn in relation to the concept of racism. Students then created their own posters that represented their ideas about racism, using the vocabulary terms identified in the original mapping activity.

In general, the steps for concept mapping are as follows:

1. Select a key concept.
2. Display the key concept and ask students to brainstorm words that relate to the concept.
3. Generate categories around words and create the map.
4. Continue to use the concept map by leading discussions that identify varied meanings and uses of key words, expand themes, and draw conclusions. Students can also extend the use of concept maps by completing projects such as the racism posters discussed above, using them as a study guide for tests or as a reference when learning new concepts.

For younger children, it is often helpful to provide headings to guide the development of categories in a concept map. For example, heading guides for the concept *weather* might include *precipitation*, *measurement*, and *patterns*. Older students may be more adept at brainstorming terms and then classifying them into categories with the help of the teacher. Figure 3.4 gives an example of a concept map created for the term *arachnid*.

• Methods for comparing and contrasting provide another way to extend understanding of key vocabulary around a theme or concept. Students can create Venn diagrams that compare and contrast two or more concepts. See Figure 3.5 for an example of a Venn diagram using the terms *cruelty* and *oppression*.

Concept maps, Venn diagrams, and other concept representations are widely used in classrooms to frame student understanding of a variety of curricular objectives. However, the focus in terms of vocabulary instruction is to develop an understanding of the key words associated with these important concepts. For example, a Venn diagram might be used to compare and contrast two novels that students have read on colonial America. A different Venn diagram or other concept representation (or possibly the same one) might be created to highlight and discuss specific terms associated with colonial America and the study of history, in general, that are essential to student understanding.

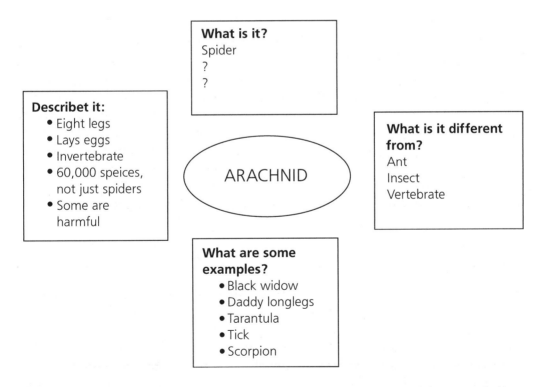

FIGURE 3.4. Partially completed concept map. Students originally thought that an *arachnid* was a spider. After completing an introductory reading, the map was expanded to include other species (e.g., tick, daddy longlegs, scorpion) with more detailed information on each. From there, the class divided into groups, which each selected a species to research further.

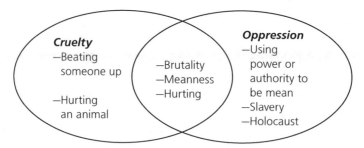

FIGURE 3.5. Venn diagram: *cruelty* versus *oppression.*

Teaching Strategies for Independent Word Learning

Independent word-learning strategies are techniques that teachers can model to their students and support their use by providing opportunities to practice with feedback. Word-learning strategies include (1) efficient use of dictionaries, thesauri, and online word resources; (2) analyzing word parts (prefixes, suffixes, roots, and compounds); and (3) using context clues to identify the meaning of unknown words. Each of these word learning strategies is discussed separately.

Efficient Use of Resources

Looking up a new vocabulary word and writing down the dictionary definition are a common, but often misused, classroom practice. The dictionary is of no use if it does not assist a student in understanding what a word means. Teaching students how to understand the abbreviations, italics, and common format of dictionary definitions, having a variety of dictionaries on hand at different levels, and allowing students to create their own dictionaries of new words with definitions, parts of speech, and example sentences help them learn to use this valuable tool. Likewise, using a thesaurus to find words that are synonyms and antonyms of vocabulary words, or even using Internet resources, can be valuable activities when students are provided with instruction on how to find and use information specific to the source.

Word Analysis Skills

There is growing support for the use of morphemic or word analysis skills in word learning. For example, fifth graders at varying skill levels were taught word analysis skills that increased their word learning in social studies (Baumann, Edwards, Boland, Olejnik, & Kame'enui, 2003). However, the authors of this study caution that because this skill only transfers to novel words that contain the specific affixes that have been taught, it should be used as one of several strategies that can be accessed by students when they come upon a word they do not know. Instruction involves teaching word-part meanings and skills for breaking apart words and putting the pieces together to come up with meanings of unknown words.

Of the various components of words to analyze, prefixes are perhaps the most worthwhile to teach because although they are present in a large number of words, there are relatively few to teach and learn, their spelling is fairly consistent, and they are always found at the beginning of a word (Graves, 2004). In fact, 20 prefixes account for 97% of words with prefixes in English (White, Sowell, & Yanagihara, 1989). For example, the prefix *dis-* means "apart or not"; *dis*respect means "not respected." There are a few drawbacks to prefixes as well. First, some words begin with prefix spellings but are not used as prefixes. For example, *pre* means *before* in the word *predetermined* but not in the word *present*. Also, some word roots do not mean anything or have a different meaning without the prefix, so having knowledge of the prefix still does not assist the reader in understanding the unknown word. This is the case in the word *invert* in which the Latin root *vert*, meaning to turn, is little help unless you are familiar with Latin. Graves (2000) suggests not teaching the use of prefixes in cases where root words are not recognizable English words. Although the reader should not be limited to teaching prefixes as part of word analysis skills, prefixes are a logical place to start. See Figure 3.6 for a list of commonly used prefixes.

Un-	Not, opposite of	Unwilling, unmanagable
Re-	Again	Return, redo
In-, im-, ir-, ill-	Not	Inaccurate, immaculate, irresponsible, illigitimate
Dis-	Not, opposite of	Disagree, disrespectful
En-, em-	Cause to	Enable, embrace
Non-	Not	Nonsense
In-	In or into	Inside, interior
Over-	Too much	Overuse
Mis-	Wrongly	Misinterpret, misunderstand
Sub-	Under	Subway, subterranean
Pre-	Before	Prehistoric, preschool
Inter-	Between	Interstate
Fore-	Before	Forefront
De-	Opposite of	Deconstruct
Trans-	Across	Transportation
Super-	Above	Superpower
Semi-	Half	Semifinal, semicircle
Anti-	Against	Antifreeze
Mid-	Middle	Midsection, midsize
Under-	Too little	Undercooked

FIGURE 3.6. Common prefixes. Adapted from Vaughn and Linan-Thompson (2004) and White, Sowell, and Yanagihara (1989).

Context Clues

Often we can figure out the meaning of a word by relating it to the text that surrounds it. The clues can be examples, contrasts, definitions, or restatements that provide some information about a word's meaning. Teaching students to successfully use context clues is a process that requires careful modeling, scaffolding, and a great deal of practice, especially for struggling readers (Beck et al., 2002). Effective use of context clues involves making connections between the known meaning of the text and the unknown word. For example, in collaborative strategic reading (described in more detail in Chapter 6) students are taught to employ such strategies as rereading the sentence and looking for clues or rereading the sentence before and after the unknown word (Klingner, Vaughn, Dimino, Schumm, & Bryant, 2001). Note that the understanding gained from a context clue is likely to be low on the "word knowing" continuum discussed earlier and will require additional and varied experiences to gain a deeper understanding of the new word (Beck, McKeown, & Omanson, 1987). Here is another strategy that has improved students' ability to use context clues to find the meaning of unknown words (Beck et al., 2002). Over time, students go from teacher-led discussions to internalizing this strategy when they come across unknown words in their reading. Consider the following passage containing the unknown word, *unsatisfactory*.

> First, Maggie missed the school bus and then she ripped a hole in her new tights when she fell off the swing at recess. Later, as she went to line up for lunch, she realized she had left her lunchbox on the kitchen table. It was not even noon, but already Maggie considered the day **unsatisfactory** in every respect.

Now apply the following steps to enact this word-learning strategy:

1. *Read and paraphrase*: The teacher or student reads the passage with the unknown word (target passage) and then restates the passage. Initially, the teacher paraphrases the passage, but students should take over this step as they become more familiar with the strategy.

2. *Establish the context*: Students are taught to ask and answer questions such as, "What is going on?" or "What is this passage about?" Again, when students are first learning this step, the teacher guides the questioning and probes responses until the student is able to correctly describe the context.

3. *Initial identification and support*: The student is asked to state what the word could mean and to provide support from the context for his or her choice. "What do you think *unsatisfactory* might mean?" The teacher asks probing questions such as "Why do you think that?" You may have to restate the context and then ask again for possible word meanings

4. *Other options*: In this step, the student is asked to generate other plausible word meanings and to defend his or her choices. Students are encouraged to consider several options because there isn't always one correct word meaning. Stu-

dents are asked, "What else might *unsatisfactory* mean?" and then, "Can you think of any other meanings?"

5. *Summarize*: In the final step, the student is asked to put all of the information together. In this way, the student learns to reflect on the contextual information that might be used to find the meaning of an unknown word. Consider the following summary conversation.

> TEACHER: So what might *unsatisfactory* mean?
>
> STUDENT: Maggie had a bad day.
>
> TEACHER: *Unsatisfactory* means bad day?
>
> STUDENT: She thought it was bad or terrible—at least, not like how things are supposed to be because she got hurt and missed her bus and stuff.
>
> TEACHER: So *unsatisfactory* might mean bad or terrible or not like how things are supposed to be. You're right. *Unsatisfactory* means not acceptable or "not like how things are supposed to be." Maggie felt that her day was unsatisfactory or unacceptable because of all of the bad things that happened to her.

In the final step, the student is also encouraged to recognize when contextual information does not provide clues to word meanings and to try another strategy when that is the case. For example, the following passage does not provide useful information about the meaning of the word *conspicuous*.

> It was late afternoon. There was no reason to think that she was conspicuous as she walked along the sidewalk. She took a key from her pocket and unlocked the door.

The independent use of strategies such as using a dictionary, word parts, or context clues requires both the ability to recognize that a word is unknown as well as the knowledge of specific strategies that could be used to help find its meaning. To make the most of these strategies, teachers need to have a thorough understanding of students' abilities to use learning strategies as well as their vocabulary knowledge and reading proficiency.

Giving Students the Opportunity to Read a Variety of Texts

Although the amount of words that students need to learn may seem daunting, promoting student engagement with text is a pleasurable and important way to increase word learning, and more importantly, leads to increased comprehension of what students read. Put simply, the amount that students read is related to the number of words they know and, in turn, allows them to read and understand increasingly complex text (Cunningham & Stanovich, 1991; Hirsch, 2003). For young children, teachers can read to students from texts that are selected based on their interest level, concepts, and vocabulary. Read-alouds are followed by engaging students in discussion that fosters understanding of the content of what was read, helps students make connections to background knowledge, supports the development or expansion of target concepts, and increases the acquisition of new vocabulary words. Remember that students enjoy and learn from read-alouds on various topics; teachers need not overrely on fiction (Hirsch, 2003) when reading to students. Magazine or newspaper articles, technical books, and other nonfiction resources are especially valuable in promoting vocabulary development, especially when several different resources are read on one theme or concept. Storybook reading (Hickman, Pollard-Durodola, & Vaughn, 2004) is a technique that uses read-alouds specifically to build vocabulary. Storybook reading can also be used with older students who are able to read the selected books or passages independently. In applying this strategy, consider the following steps:

1. Choose a high-interest book that contains key vocabulary or concepts. You may want to select a short passage or read just a few pages each day, depending on the length of the book.
2. Before reading, select a few difficult words and give simple definitions using familiar language. Write down the words and definitions (e.g., *flee: to run away*).
3. During reading, tell students to listen for the vocabulary words (or to look for the key vocabulary if they are reading) and encourage them to use clues in the story to find out what the words mean.
4. After reading, engage students in a discussion about the story and the key words. Ask questions to help students *explain* and *describe* what has been read. Encourage students to describe how the key words were used and how they fit into core ideas of the text. You may also ask students to use the new vocabulary to summarize or retell the story or passage.

Providing rich and varied reading experiences around key concepts increases the acquisition of new vocabulary words as well as the "world knowledge" that is needed to connect the words with the text in order to improve reading comprehension (Hirsch, 2003).

Increasing Students' Knowledge of, and Interest in Words

Throughout this chapter we have providing examples of activities that allow students to actively engage in word learning—to play with words, to think about words, and to become interested in words and their many and varied uses. This notion of developing *word consciousness* is supported by research (e.g., Anderson & Nagy, 1992; Beck & McKeown, 1983; Scott & Nagy, 2004) and occurs through meaningful vocabulary activities.

Language play is another way to increase students' interest in words and to facilitate the production and understanding of language. Teachers and students can create all sorts of games, including memory games, crossword puzzles, codes, word scrambles, guessing games, bingo, charades, tongue twisters, alliteration, letter games, and categories that challenge students to play with, discover, remember, and develop an appreciation of how words are used. The following list divides word play into seven categories that provide a springboard for a multitude of word games (adapted from Johnson, Johnson, & Schlichting, 2004):

- *Onomastics* is the study of names. Students are encouraged to think about names, their origins, why certain names are given (*Maple Street, a dog named Woof, a cat named Princess*), and to look at the meaning of, and play on, words that are common in names (*Comeback Inn, For Eyes*).
- *Expressions* include idioms (*hang on*), proverbs ("Don't count your chickens before they've hatched"), slang (*decked out*), catchphrases (24/7), and slogans.
- *Figures of speech* are words that are not used literally but suggest another meaning. Examples include similes (*as big as a whale*), metaphors (the rainbow is beauty), hyperbole ("I cried a thousand tears"), euphemisms ("temporarily displaced"—*stolen*), and oxymorons (*cruel kindness*).
- *Word associations* are recognized ways to connect words to each other, such as synonyms (*ugly, unattractive*), antonyms (*huge, tiny*), homographs (*desert, desert*), and homophones (*plane, plain*).
- *Word formations* include acronyms (*USDA*), compounds (*backyard*), and affixes (*neo-, -ing*).
- *Word manipulations* play with letters and include anagrams (*mane, name*), palindromes (*bird rib*), and rebuses (I &〜 U).
- *Ambiguities* are words, phrases, or sentences that are open to more than one interpretation (*Robber gets 6 months in violin case*).

CONCLUSION

Understanding words in all their complexity is an essential part of comprehending text. Although important in all grades and across all genres, understanding word meaning is particularly important after second grade and with expository text. As students encounter more challenging words and concepts, assisting them in understanding and learning from text requires effective practices for teaching vocabulary. Students who are "word conscious"—that is, they pay attention to words they don't know and strive to learn more about those words—are likely to reap the benefits of improved word and concept knowledge. Perhaps the most important outcome of improved vocabulary is improved comprehension.

VOCABULARY SAMPLE LESSON PLANS
(to Accompany Chapter 3)

CLICK AND CLUNK[1]

Note: Click and Clunk is one of the strategies used in the multicomponent strategy instruction, collaborative strategic reading, described in Chapter 6. "Clunks" are words students do not understand.

Grade Levels

Third grade and up

Purpose

Students learn to use fix-up strategies to figure out the meaning of unknown words during reading.

Materials

Reading passage
Cue cards with fix-up strategies

Lesson

1. *Introduce clunks and fix-up strategies using short examples.*

- Clunks are words or concepts that students do not understand and that impair comprehension of a passage. Model how to use fix-up strategies using a sample sentence and the fix-up strategy cue cards.

A snake's body is very *supple*. It can bend easily. It can fit in small spaces.

- Use the clunk cards to determine the meaning of the word *supple*. In this case, clunk card 2, "Reread the sentence before and after the clunk and look for clues," provides the fix-up strategy that helps students figure out the meaning of the clunk word, *supple*.
- Have students work in pairs to use fix-up strategies to find the meaning of the clunks in the following examples, or create examples that are appropriate to your students' reading levels.

---

[1]Click and Clunk adapted from Klingner et al. (2001). Copyright 2001 by Sopris West. Adapted by permission.

---

1. In the summer the birds *molt*, or lose their feathers.

2. You can find out how to make good food in a *cookbook*.
3. The *falcon* is a hunting bird.

4. The falcon has a *hooked beak* and strong *talons*.
5. The moose has big *antlers*.

2. *Apply the fix-up strategies to longer passages.*

- Identify two or three "clunks" in the passage. Read the passage out loud to students (students should follow along with their own passage or on the overhead).
- Model how to use the fix-up strategies to identify which strategy might help figure out the meaning of the unknown word or idea. Repeat this process for another clunk.
- Write down each clunk and a brief definition.
- Have students work with a partner or small group to practice using the fix-up strategies to find the meaning clunks. One student can be a "clunk" expert and hold the clunk cards. After reading a section of the passage (usually a paragraph or two of a content-area or other expository text, depending on the length and difficulty of the reading passage), students stop to identify clunks.
- The clunk expert reads the first clunk card, and the student who had the clunk attempts to use it to find the meaning. Students can assist each other with using fix-up strategies. If one student knows the definition of a word, using the fix-up strategies should confirm the definition.

Fix-Up Strategies

#1 Reread the sentence without the clunk and ask what word would make sense in its place.	#2 Reread the sentence before and after the clunk and look for clues.
#3 Break the word apart and look for smaller words you know.	#4 Look for a prefix or suffix in the word that might help

3. *Use other resources if the fix-up strategies don't work.*

- Sometimes students use the fix-up strategies but still can't figure out the meaning of word. You should create a system for what to do next. Examples include the following:

- ✓ If the fix-up strategies don't work, one student raises his or her hand and waits for the teacher.
- ✓ If the fix-up strategies don't work, put the word/concept on the "Challenge Chart." The teacher can then address the challenge words or concepts when the group comes back together.
- ✓ If the fix-up strategies don't work, continue with the reading assignment and use an accepted classroom resource (dictionary, computer) once you have finished.

4. *Review clunks with the class.*

- Check the clunks students identify. You may need to provide additional instruction for clunks with which many students seem to be struggling as well as those clunks that are very important for students to know well.

Adaptation for Students with Special Needs

If students are not able to use fix-up strategies to find the meaning of clunks, check the following:

- Be sure that students understand the fix-up strategies and how to use them. You may need to provide additional practice with short examples until students are comfortable with the strategies.
- Sometimes students do not identify clunks because they are not aware of what they *do not* understand. In this case, begin by identifying the clunks. For example, you might say, "While you are reading the next section, look for the clunks *viscosity* and *permeable.* Use the fix-up strategies to find the meaning of the clunks and write down a brief definition on your clunk list."
- Students benefit from working in pairs or small heterogeneous groups to read and use fix-up strategies. If students are having difficulty applying the fix-up strategies, pay attention to how they are grouped so that all group members are engaged and actively participating.
- If students have too many clunks, the fix-up strategies may not help. In this case more explicit preteaching of vocabulary may be necessary. Also, consider using lower-level reading material.

VOCABULARY CUE CARDS[2]

Grade Levels

Intermediate and upper grade levels

Purpose

Students actively engage in deepening their understanding of vocabulary words when they create their own study aids.

Materials

Reading passage
Cue cards

[2]Vocabulary Cue Cards adapted from Davis (1990).

Dictionary, thesaurus, or computer
Vocabulary list

Lesson

1. *Students work in pairs to complete "cue cards" for their vocabulary words.*

- Explain: *"TV news anchors use cue cards to help them remember what to say. You are going to make your own cue cards to help you remember the meaning of vocabulary words."*
- Have students work with a partner to create cue cards for important vocabulary words. On one side of the cue card write the word. On the other side, write the word, a brief definition, examples, and nonexamples:

Word:	
Definition:	
Examples: 1. 2. 3.	Nonexamples: 1. 2. 3.

3. *Have a cue card competition.*

- Bring the pairs together into two teams.
- Agree on an acceptable definition of the word.
- Then alternate between teams to create a list of examples and nonexamples. Each team gets 1 point for a correct example or nonexample shared by the other team and 2 points for a correct example or nonexample that the other team does not have. After reaching a predetermined number of examples (five or ten), continue with the next word.
- During the game, evaluate student responses and provide feedback to ensure that students are developing a correct understanding of each word.

Adaptation for Students with Special Needs

- Use a base list and add additional words for students who need enrichment or for those who are struggling. For example, most of the class works on the same ten vocabulary words. Several students have five essential words from the class list and five (or fewer) more basic words with which they are struggling. Several other students have the five essential words and five enrichment words.
- Shorten the list for students who may not be able to thoughtfully complete the list within the given time frame.
- Vary the amount of information provided on the cue card. For some students, you might provide the vocabulary word and the definition, and the student's task is to come up with examples and nonexamples.
- Students who work slowly can provide only one example and nonexample on their cue cards.
- Students who struggle with writing can create cue cards on a computer or have the abler partner do the writing.

SEMANTIC MAPS

Grade Levels

All

Purpose

Create a semantic map to show how words that relate to a key concept are connected to each other.

Materials

Semantic mapping chart, chalk board, or overhead

Lesson

1. *Brainstorm words associated with a key concept.*

- As a class, have students brainstorm all the words that are associated with a key concept or idea. You may also have several key words that you would like to highlight, and you can add them to the class list.

2. *Create a semantic map.*

- Now group related words and create category headings. Visually represent the relationship between the categories and the key concept on a semantic map. Once students have practiced creating whole-class semantic maps, they can work individually, in pairs, or in small groups to categorize words and identify relationships related to a key concept.

3. *Extend the activity.*

- Students can use semantic maps as a previewing activity prior to reading, to review important vocabulary and key ideas, or as a starting point for writing an essay or research paper.

CHAPTER 4

Text Structure
and Reading Comprehension

STUDY GROUP PROMPTS

1. Before reading this chapter, think about what you already know about text structure. Now think about what you know about ways to teach different text structures. Ask members of your study group how they are currently teaching their students about text structure. Make a list of these practices.

2. As you read, think about which practices for enhancing students' understanding and use of text structures you already implement with your students. Are there new practices you would like to add to your repertoire?

3. After reading this chapter, discuss with your study group what you learned about narrative and expository text structures and how this information might help you support your students' reading comprehension. Revisit the list of text structure practices you developed before reading and consider whether you would revise these practices in any way.

4. Select an expository or informational passage and discuss ways to expose its text structure for students so that they might find learning from text easier. Plan a lesson for this purpose.

"Once upon a time _____ _____ _____ _____ _____. . . . " Fill in the blanks. What words came to mind? You probably thought of something like "there were three little pigs." Or maybe you thought "there was a princess who lived in a castle in a land far away." You expect to hear a story in which the characters and setting will be described and a problem will unfold. The story will have a hero or heroine and a villain and a problem to be solved. You expect to find out how the hero will prevail. You would be very surprised if at the end of the story you were not informed that everyone "lived happily ever after." In Western culture this is a typical and very familiar narrative text structure. Young children grow up hearing fairy tales and other stories that help them learn this story grammar. They learn what to expect next when listening to or reading a story. A schema has been activated. Think of a schema as a template or framework in the mind that is called up when needed. This schema is based on prior knowledge. When we lack a schema or the schema is incomplete, our comprehension is hindered. On the other hand, a complete schema facilitates comprehension as well as memory. When we retell or summarize a story, this template provides an organizing structure that helps us do this more efficiently (Kintsch & Greene, 1978).

As you read, think about various text structures and how they influence reading comprehension. The first text structure that most of us use is narrative (i.e., fiction). We also learn expository text structures (i.e., factual and informational). In this chapter we examine both structures with a focus on students with LD. We also describe numerous teaching strategies for helping students learn to use text structures to their advantage.

What is *text structure*? This term refers to the way a text is organized to guide readers in identifying key information. Texts are organized in different ways. Narrative text typically follows a single, general, structural pattern, often called a story grammar (Mandler & Johnson, 1977). Story grammar includes characters, setting, problems, and solutions to the problems. Expository text comes in a variety of different organizational patterns (described later in this chapter). Some texts are written with more reader-friendly text structures than others (Pearson & Dole, 1987). When students are familiar with the way a text is structured, this knowledge can help them (1) form expectations about what they will read, (2) organize incoming information, (3) judge the relative importance of what they read, (4) improve their comprehension, and (5) enhance their recall (Meyer, 1984). However, when the structure of a text is different from what the reader expects, comprehension can break down. Struggling readers are more likely than stronger readers to be unaware of text structures and to experience difficulty using them to help with comprehension (e.g., Meyer, Brandt, & Bluth, 1980). Yet explicit instruction can help struggling readers become more aware of various text structures and augment their comprehension and memory (Dickson, Simmons, & Kame'enui, 1995; Gersten, Fuchs, Williams, & Baker, 2001; Goldman & Rakestraw, 2000; Meyer, 1984; Ohlhausen & Roller, 1988).

TEXT STRUCTURE AND STUDENTS WITH LEARNING DISABILITIES

Many students with LD process information inefficiently. They may be unaware of simple strategies that good readers use automatically, such as rereading passages they do not understand (Williams, 2000). Students with LD are often confused by different forms of text structure and may have trouble keeping track of various ways stories can be structured. Their lack of knowledge interferes with their comprehension and memory. Students with LD typically recall less about stories they have read and cannot easily identify the important information in them (Roth & Speckman, 1986). In fact, Cain (1996) found that students with LD had less knowledge of story structure than younger children (Cain, 1996). Gersten et al. (2001) speculated that the narrative comprehension difficulties of students with LD may be a result of a breakdown in metacognition—in other words, not being able to reflect on how reading is progressing, or not knowing which strategies to use when there is a breakdown in understanding. Expository text structures, such as those found in history books or periodicals, can present students with LD with even greater challenges than narrative text structures. Expository text structures can take many different forms, and it can be difficult for students with LD to figure out which form is being used. The knowledge and tactics best suited for understanding these different forms of text structure vary. In contrast, good readers are better able to discern which structure is being used and to determine which strategies to apply to aid their comprehension.

NARRATIVE STORY STRUCTURE

Children develop sensitivity to narrative structure early. By the time they begin school, most children have developed some sense of story structure and can use this knowledge to comprehend simple stories (Gillis & Olson, 1987). As noted, the structure of narratives is often called a "story grammar." This term refers to the different elements the reader can expect to find in a story, such as the characters, setting, plot (including a problem that needs to be solved), and a resolution to the problem. Narratives include different types, or genres, that can vary somewhat from this basic story grammar template. These include realistic fiction, fantasy, fairytales, folktales, fables, mysteries, humor, historical fiction, plays, and real-life adventures. For example, fables are short stories with a typical story grammar but with the addition of a moral. Readers remember stories better when they are organized in familiar ways (Mandler & DeForest, 1979; Stein & Nezworski, 1978).

As students mature, their understanding of different stories becomes more sophisticated (Williams, 2000). Many students develop a keen understanding of how stories are structured without every receiving explicit story grammar instruction. However, students with LD are slower to develop this ability. They may not be good at certain tasks, such as selecting important information, making inferences, and identifying story themes. Students with poor comprehension, who may not have developed this understanding on their own, can benefit from explicit instruction (Idol, 1987; Goldman & Rakestraw, 2000; Pearson & Fielding, 1991). Several studies have addressed the question of how to improve the ability of students with LD to use narrative structure. Williams (2000) noted that most research on narrative text has focused on teaching students to utilize story structure as an organizing framework for understanding critical aspects of the stories they read. For example, Idol (1987) taught story mapping to heterogeneous groups of third and fourth graders and found that low- and average-achieving students not only improved in their ability to answer questions about stories they had just read, but also improved in listening comprehension, criterion-referenced tests, and spontaneous story writing.

Cultural Variation

Have you ever listened to a story and wished that the storyteller would stop going around in circles and just get to the point? Perhaps you grew impatient because you wanted to know how a problem was resolved. Or maybe you found yourself wanting to know more details about the characters and their emotions and relationships with one another. You may even have felt annoyed when the storyteller did not provide them. These differences reflect variations in narrative text structures across cultures. The storytelling styles of diverse cultural groups emphasize and value different parts of a story. For example, the traditional white, middle-class structure tends to be "topic-centered." The emphasis is on getting the sequence of events correct and on being clear. Stories in the Latino culture often deemphasize the importance of structure and action and emphasize emotions and family connections (McCabe, 1995). Traditional Native American stories typically have no clear ending because they are about life, and life has no ending (Cazden, 1988). Thus, some black, Latino, or Native American students may not emphasize the mainstream topic-centered approach to stories or chronologically sequence story events (Cazden, 1988; Champion, 1997; McCabe, 1995; Michaels, 1981). Rather, their stories often link episodes in a topic-associative way and focus on human relationships (McCabe, 1995).

These unique cultural patterns affect students' understanding and recall of a story (Bean, Potter, & Clark, 1980; Carrell, 1984) as well as the type of information recalled (high- versus low-level; Carrell, 1984, 1992). In general, passages organized in a familiar structure are easier to comprehend and remember than passages structured in a less familiar way (Carrell, 1984; Hinds, 1983; Fitzgerald, 1995). Invernizz and Abouzeid (1995) studied the story recall of sixth graders in New Guinea and Virginia. Both groups of students had been taught in English with Western-style textbooks. Students were asked to read two stories with different narrative structures. As expected, both groups recalled more about the story closest to the text structure most common in their culture. New Guinea children recalled more of the setting and details but often omitted the moral, whereas American students focused on general points of the story as well as the consequences and resolutions. Similarly, McClure, Mason, and Williams (1983) examined how black, white, and Latino working- and middle-class students in the United States unscrambled different versions of a text and found that students performed the best on stories most typical in their cultural background.

Though text structures are generally learned implicitly through repeated exposure to and practice with stories, explicit instruction in different structures can help students learn them. For example, Amer (1992) found that direct instruction in text structure facilitated the comprehension and recall of sixth-grade students studying

English as a foreign language. Goldstone (2002) noted that students need concrete, specific information about the special features and organization of picture books to enhance their appreciation and comprehension. Students from diverse ethnic backgrounds who also have LD may experience challenges when trying to understand different text structures. They would benefit from instruction that values their perspectives and storytelling traditions and also teaches the conventional story grammar typically used in U.S. schools.

Teaching Strategies

In this section of the chapter, we describe numerous strategies and techniques that can help students with LD learn about story grammars. Some procedures focus on providing students with an organizational guide to use when reading that includes the principal components of a story (e.g., main character, setting, action, and outcome). Other activities draw students' attention to different story elements. Some techniques prompt students to apply different comprehension strategies designed to facilitate their understanding of text. Many researchers who have developed strategies for enhancing students understanding of narrative text structure emphasize the connection between reading and writing (e.g., Baker, Gersten, & Graham, 2003; Irwin & Baker, 1989). Additional ideas for teaching text structure can be found in the lesson plans at the end of this chapter.

Story Maps

Visual representations such as story maps can be beneficial for all students, and are especially helpful for students with LD (Baker et al., 2003). Story maps take numerous forms. One variation we like is the organization sheet developed by Englert (1990, 1992) to help students plan for writing; the topic or title of the story is written in a circle in the middle of the page and the subtopics or components of the plot are written in the surrounding circles. We have added the C-SPACE mnemonic device for helping students remember the elements of a story (C-characters, S-setting, P-problem, A-action, C-conclusion, E-emotion) (MacArthur, Schwartz, & Graham, 1991; MacArthur, Graham, Schwartz, & Schafer, 1995) (see Figure 4.1).

Story Face

The "story face" is an adaptation of story mapping that provides a visual framework for understanding, identifying, and remembering elements in narrative text (Staal, 2000). Staal described several strengths of the story face strategy when used with students in first through fifth grades: It (1) is easy to construct, (2) is easy to remember, (3) can guide retelling, (4) is collaboratively learned through discovery, (5) is flexible, and (6) provides a framework that can facilitate narrative writing. It looks like a story map, only it is shaped like a face. Staal provides examples of "happy" and "sad" faces. We offer an adaptation of the happy version (for the sad face, the smile is upside down) (see Figure 4.2).

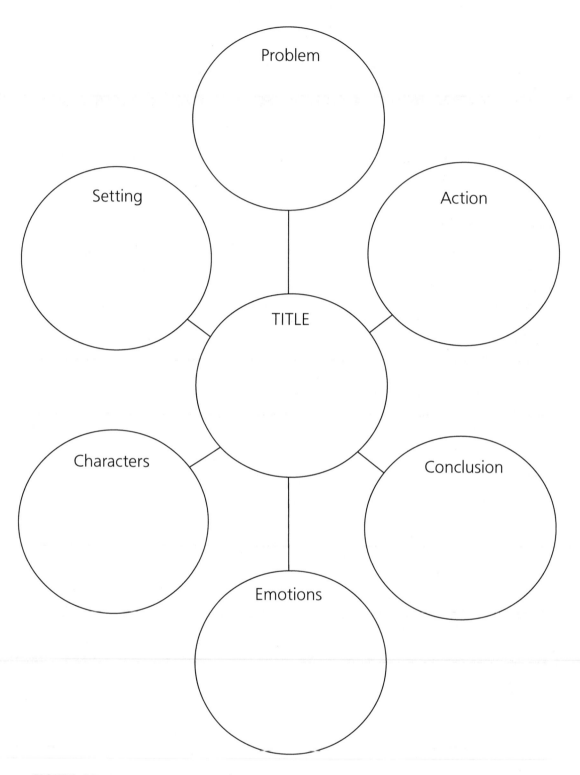

FIGURE 4.1. Story map with C-SPACE. From Haager and Klingner (2005). Copyright 2005 by Pearson Education. Reprinted by permission.

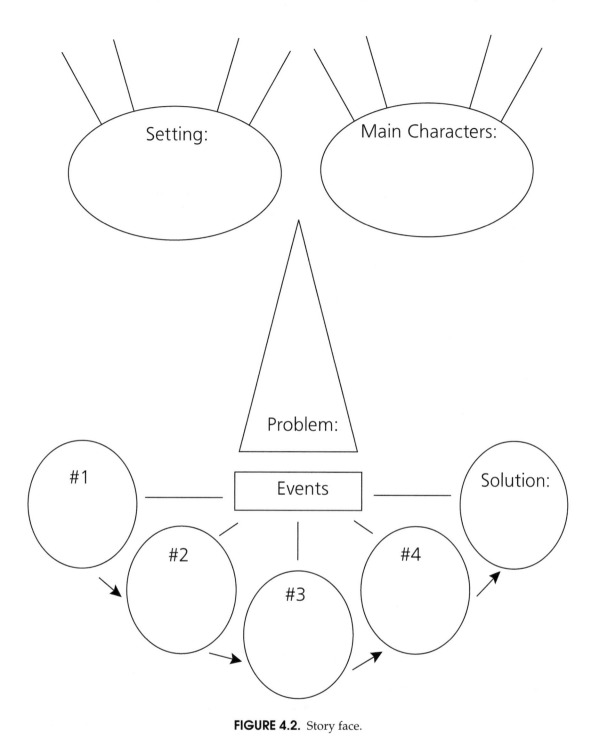

FIGURE 4.2. Story face.

Story Gloves

Story gloves prompt students to use the comprehension strategies associated with different text structures (Newman, 2001–2002). The gloves provide visual clues through icons on each finger and in the palm. Newman described three different gloves: the prereading glove, the narrative text structure glove, and the expository text structure glove. Each glove has five questions to guide students' discussions, with little objects or pictures to remind students which questions to answer. Teachers can vary the icons to better match students' ages. The narrative text structure glove includes the following icons and questions:

1. *Plane*: "Where does the story take place?"
2. *Animal/person*: "Who are the characters?"
3. *Stairs*: "What happened first? Next? Last?"
4. *Chalkboard with "1 + 1"*: "What was the problem in the story?"
5. *Chalkboard with "2"*: "What was the story's (re)solution?"

Story Recipe

The connections between reading and writing are strong. Irwin and Baker (1989) note that teaching students to write stories using a template or graphic organizer can improve their understanding of story grammar and facilitate their comprehension when they read stories. They promote a graphic organizer called a "story recipe" (see Figure 4.3). The story recipe format can be used as a tool to help students construct stories by having them complete each part of the recipe prior to writing, as a planning sheet. Or it can be completed after students read a story as an exercise for analyzing story structure. We present an original story, "Randy Raindrop" (Figure 4.4) and then illustrate how we used the story recipe format to examine the structure of the story (Figure 4.5).

Retelling

Retelling is a commonly used procedure that involves asking students to recall and restate the events in a story after they have read it or heard it (e.g., "What happened first? What happened next?"). Morrow (1986) developed a version of retelling to provide kindergarten students with structural guidance to improve their sense of story structure. She recommended first modeling the different parts of story for students (e.g., starting a story by saying "once upon a time"), and then prompting students to retell the story by asking:

- Who was the story about?
- Where did the story happen (or take place)?
- What was the main character's problem?
- How did the main character try to solve the problem?
- How did the story end?

Main characters	
Names	Traits

Setting	
Where?	Description

Plot outline			
Beginning event	Problem	How the character felt	What he or she did

Conclusion	
Consequences—How did it end?	Is there a moral to the story?

FIGURE 4.3. Story recipe. From Irwin and Baker (1989). Copyright 1989 by Pearson Education. Reprinted by permission.

Randy Raindrop

Once upon a time there was a little raindrop named Randy. Randy lived in a big, white, fluffy cloud with his parents, Raymond and Rita. He loved to play with other little raindrops. But sometimes he and his friends wandered far away from their parents. Their parents warned them to stay close by. One day when Randy was playing hide and go seek with his friends, he went too far. Then the big cloud got dark. There was a loud BOOM and a flash of light, and the cloud shook. Randy tried to hurry back to his parents, but he was too far away. He stumbled and fell out of his cloud. Down, down he fell, until he landed with a splash on the ground. He got up and looked around. He didn't know where he was, and he didn't know any of the other raindrops he saw. He was scared and sad. He missed his parents! He thought, "I should have listened to them and stayed closer!" More and more raindrops fell to the ground around Randy. Then Randy started moving, faster and faster, with the other raindrops around him. They rolled down a hill and into a river. The river was flowing quickly, rushing and gushing. Randy thought he would never stop, but finally the river slowed down and Randy was able to look around him. And who did he see? His parents! They had also fallen out of the cloud, and had been looking for him. Randy and his parents were so happy to be together again! They gave Randy a big hug, and Randy promised to do a better job following their directions.

FIGURE 4.4. Original story: "Randy Raindrop."

Main characters	
Names	Traits
Randy Raindrop	He likes to play with other raindrops.

Setting	
Where?	Description
1. A cloud 2. The ground and a river	1. The cloud is big, white, and fluffy at first, but then becomes dark. 2. The river moves quickly.

Plot outline			
Beginning event	Problem	How the character felt	What he or she did
Randy is playing with his friends and goes too far from his parents.	The cloud shakes and Randy falls to the ground. He is lost.	He feels sad and scared.	He and other raindrops flow into a river. The river flows fast.

Conclusion	
Consequences—How did it end?	Is there a moral to the story?
Randy finds his parents.	Yes. It's best to do what your parents say.

FIGURE 4.5. Completed story recipe, using "Randy Raindrop."

TELLS

Idol-Maestas (1985) developed an approach called TELLS for guiding students' probing while reading a story. TELLS is an acronym that prompts students to follow a series of steps:

- T: study story titles.
- E: examine and skim pages for clues.
- L: look for important words.
- L: look for difficult words.
- S: think about the story settings.

TELLS can be posted on a wall in the classroom and/or provided individually to students. The teacher helps students learn how to apply each of the steps, one at a time, and then use them all when reading a story. Idol-Maestas (1985) suggested that it is important to continue prompting students to use this and other comprehension strategies even after they appear to have become proficient in strategy implementation. Explicit instruction using transfer activities to help students internalize strategies and generalize their usage to other tasks is important, especially for students with LD.

Theme Scheme

Williams (2005) provided at-risk primary-grade children with explicit instruction in different text structure strategies and found that their comprehension improved and that they were able to transfer the strategies they learned to novel texts. The first approach she investigated was the "Theme Scheme," includes the following steps:

- *Introduction and prereading discussion*: In the first part of the lesson, the teacher defines the concept of theme, discusses the value of understanding themes, and introduces the background of the specific story for that lesson.
- *Reading the story*: The teacher reads the story aloud, interspersing the text with questions designed to encourage students to process the text actively (e.g., make connections with prior knowledge).
- *Discussion using organizing (theme scheme) questions*: The teacher and students discuss eight questions.

1. Who is the main character?
2. What is the main character's problem?
3. What did the main character do about the problem (solution)?
4. And then what happened?
5. Was that good or bad?
6. Why was it good or bad?

7. The main character learned that he or she should _____.
8. We should _____.

• *Transfer and application of the theme to other story examples and to real-life experiences*: The teacher introduces a one-paragraph vignette that provides another example of the same theme. The teacher and students discuss the example using the eight questions, plus two additional questions:

1. When is it important to _____?
2. In what situation is it easy/difficult to _____?

• *Review*: The teacher reviews the eight organizing questions and asks students to think about other examples.
• *Activity*: The teacher leads the class in a follow-up enrichment activity, such as writing, drawing, discussion, or role playing.

Prediction Task

For this activity, the teacher reads a story to students or has them read a story, stopping before getting to the story's resolution (Whaley, 1981). Then the teacher asks students to predict what comes next in the unfinished story. This activity can be an open-ended, or the teacher can provide students with different possible endings from which they can choose.

Cloze Task

The teacher removes a portion of text from the middle of a story and then has students fill in the missing information (Whaley, 1981). Students can complete the activity individually, in pairs, or in small groups. To optimize the benefits of this approach, it is valuable to discuss the types of information that would be expected. For example, the teacher might remove the description of the problem faced by the characters in the story. The teacher then could show students a story map and ask them what aspect of the map is not apparent in the story. They could brainstorm possible problems that would make sense, given the other information presented in the story. A possible variation of this approach is to ask different groups to do this for various parts of a story (each changing one part) and then have students put their revised parts together to form a new (silly) story.

Scrambled Stories

For this approach, the teacher breaks a story into categories (chunks) and then mixes them up (Whaley, 1981). Next, the teacher has students put the pieces of the story back together in the right order. The teacher and students discuss which way makes the most sense and why. A variation of this technique is to use it with the language experience approach and stories students themselves have written (Haager & Klingner, 2005). Prepackaged blank sentence strips can be useful for this process.

EXPOSITORY TEXT STRUCTURE

The term *expository text structure* refers to the ways text is organized to guide readers in identifying key information and making connections among ideas. Because the structures found in content-area textbooks differ substantially from those in narrative texts, strategies students may have learned to implement with narrative prose do not necessarily transfer. For numerous reasons, expository text structures are more challenging for students than narrative structures. For one, although many children start school with an awareness of narrative text structure, few begin school with an awareness of expository text structure, in part because most parents read to their preschool children from storybooks (Williams, Hall, & Lauer, 2004). Also, the connections between ideas in expository texts are not the simple sequence of familiar events depicted in many narratives. Another reason is that expository texts appear in a variety of different organizational structures, such as (Weaver & Kintsch, 1991):

1. Enumeration—a list of facts concerning a single topic.
2. Sequence—a series of events that occur over time.
3. Compare–contrast—a focus on the similarities and differences between two or more topics.
4. Classification—information organized according to categories.
5. Generalization—one major idea contained within a few sentences.
6. Problem–solution—the statement of a problem followed by its solution.
7. Procedural description—the steps used to carry out a task.

When reading expository text, students must not only attend to the information in the text but also identify the type of text structure used to present it (Englert & Hiebert, 1984). Students with LD demonstrate less awareness of these different expository text structures than their normally achieving peers (Seidenberg, 1989). "Poor readers, including students with LD, find expository text structure particularly difficult" (Williams et al., 2004, p. 131).

An additional reason expository text structures can be so challenging is that few content-area textbooks are written in ways that make their text structure or meaning easily accessible (Harniss, Dickson, Kinder, & Hollenbeck, 2001; Jitendra et al., 2001). Most textbooks lack coherence (i.e., the connections between ideas are not readily apparent; Meyer, 2003). They are written with complex text that is difficult for students with LD to understand (Venable, 2003). History textbooks seem to be poorly organized and can be particularly challenging for teachers and students (with and without LD) to use effectively (Harniss et al., 2001). Similarly, Jitendra et al. (2001) evaluated the readability levels, knowledge forms, intellectual operations, instructional objectives, and activities in four middle school geography textbooks. Although the results varied somewhat, Jitendra and colleagues found that the texts were dense with factual information and generally were inconsiderate of struggling readers. Clues that might help students with LD were absent.

One more aspect of expository text structure merits consideration before we present teaching strategies. Just as story grammars vary by culture, so too do expository text structures. For example, not all cultures include the compare-and-contrast structure. Argument structures vary across cultures, as do ways of making a point (e.g., subtle or direct). It is important for teachers to keep this in mind so that they do not mistakenly attribute learning or cognitive disabilities to students who are more familiar with a different rhetorical style, and so that they can provide students with appropriate support as they learn new expository text structures (Fillmore & Snow, 2000).

Teaching Strategies

Numerous strategies designed to enhance expository text comprehension have been taught to students with LD, with promising results. For example, Richgels, McGee, and Slaton (1989) taught students to create visual representations to focus their attention on test structure. Dickson, Simmons, and Kame'enui (1995) helped students learn the compare–contrast text structure by teaching them to look out for signal words such as *like, different, in contrast,* and *but.* Williams (2005) conducted a series of intervention studies and concluded that at-risk children in the primary grades can achieve gains in comprehension, including the ability to transfer what they have learned to novel texts, when they are given highly structured and explicit instruction that focuses on text structure.

Identifying Text Structures

Different researchers have evaluated approaches for teaching students to identify expository text structures. We describe three here. Irwin (1991) suggested providing students with explicit instruction in text structure types and then asking them to identify the forms they find in their content-area textbooks. This approach should first be conducted using guided practice and just two contrasting text structures, subsequently adding new types until students are ready to identify text structures independently. In Table 4.1 we list five basic text organizational structures and the signals words and phrases that can serve as clues to help students identify them (adapted from Meyer et al., 1980; also in Meyer, 2003).

Armbruster and Anderson (1981) offered an alternative version of the various expository text structures (see Table 4.2). They encouraged students to think about the authors' purpose for presenting information (e.g., comparing and contrasting or describing). Along with each type of text structure, they provide examples of what the imperative form (i.e., statements) as well as interrogative form (i.e., ques-

TABLE 4.1. Five Basic Text Organizational Structures and Their Signals

Text structure	Signal words and phrases
Description	
Describes the attributes, specifics, and/or setting. The main idea is the "who, what, where, when, and how."	for example, for instance, this particular, specifically, such as, attributes of, properties of, characteristics of, qualities of, in describing
Sequence	
Groups ideas by order or time. The main idea is the procedure or sequence of events related.	first, next, then, afterward, later, last, finally, following, to begin with, to start with, as time passed, continuing on, in the end, years ago, in the first place, before, after, soon, recently
Causation	
Presents causes or cause-and-effect relationships between ideas. The main idea is organized into cause-and-effect parts.	if/then, as a result, because, since, for the purpose of, caused, led to, consequences, thus, in order to, this is why, the reason, so in explanation, therefore
Problem/solution	
Portrays a problem and solutions. The main idea is organized into two parts: a problem part and a solution part, or a question part and an answer part.	*problem*: problem, question, puzzle, enigma, riddle, hazard, issue, query, need to prevent, the trouble *solution*: solution, answer, response, reply, rejoinder, return, to satisfy the problem, to take care of the problem, in answer to the problem, to solve the problem, to set the issue at rest
Comparison	
Relates ideas on the basis of differences and similarities. The main idea is organized into parts that provide a comparison, contrast, or alternative perspectives on a topic.	*compare*: alike, have in common, share, resemble, the same as, is similar to, looks like, is like *contrast*: in contrast, but, not everyone, all but, instead, however, in comparison, on the other hand, whereas, in opposition to, unlike, differ, different, difference, differentiate, compared to, whereas, although, despite
Listing	
Occurs with any of the above structures (i.e., when descriptions, sequences, causation, problems/solutions, or comparison views are presented).	and, in addition, also, include, moreover, besides, first, second, third, subsequent, furthermore, at the same time, another

Note. Adapted from Meyer (2003). Copyright 2003 by Erlbaum. Adapted by permission.

TABLE 4.2. Types of Text Structures and Author Purposes

Structure	Imperative form	Interrogative form
Description	Define A Describe A List the features/characteristics of A	What is A? Who is A? Where is A?
Temporal sequences	Trace the development of A Give the steps in A	When did A occur (in relation to other events)?
Explanation	Explain A Explain cause(s) of A Explain the effect(s) Predict/hypothesize	Why did A happen? How did A happen? What are the effects? What will the effects be?
Compare–contrast	Compare and contrast List the similarities and differences	How are A and B alike? How are A and B different?
Definitions/examples	Define and give examples	What is A? What are examples of A?
Problem/solution	Explain the problem and the solution	How is B a problem? What are its solutions?

Note. Data from Armbruster and Anderson (1981).

tions) of each type looks like. These examples are similar to the key words and phrases suggested by Meyer et al. (1980).

Bakken and Whedon (2002) explained how to teach children with disabilities to identify five different types of expository text structures: main idea, list, order, compare–contrast, and classification. For each structure, Bakken and Whedon not only describe the structure and corresponding signals or clues that can help to identify the structure, but also the reading objective, a study strategy, and a note-taking form. Once students learn to differentiate among the various text structures, they then learn to apply appropriate structure-specific strategies (see Table 4.3).

Explicit Instruction in Individual Text Structures

Some researchers have taught students strategies to facilitate their understanding of specific text structures. For example, Armbruster, Anderson, and Ostertag (1987) provided middle school students with explicit instruction in the problem–solution structure and found that they recalled more information on an essay test and also identified more main ideas than comparison students who did not learn the structure. Ciardiello (2002) promoted question networks as a strategy to assist students in understanding cause–effect text structures in their social studies textbooks. Williams (2005) and Dickson et al. (1995) focused on the compare–contrast structure (described below).

TABLE 4.3. Text Structures, Formats, Signals, Reading Objectives, and Study Strategies

Structure	Format	Signals	Reading objective	Study Strategy
Main idea	Focus is on a single topic, with supporting details	Definitions, principles, laws	To understand the main idea and be able to explain it using supporting details.	Identify and restate the main idea. Select and list at least three supporting details.
List	Focus is on a general topic, with a list of facts or characteristics	Semicolons, numbers, or letters in parentheses	To recognize the general topic and be able to list specific characteristics.	Identify and restate the topic. Select and list at least four characteristics.
Order	Focus is on a general topic, with a connected series of events or steps in order	Words such as *first, second, third, then*	To identify the topic, describe each step in sequence, and tell the difference among steps.	Identify and restate the topic. Select and list the steps. Tell what is different from one step to the next.
Compare–contrast	Focus is on the relationships (similarities and differences) between two or more things	Phrases such as *in contrast, the difference between*	To identify the topics and discuss the similarities and/or differences.	Identify and restate the topic. Use a graphic organizer (e.g., a table with two columns, a Venn diagram) to write what is the same and/or different.
Classification	Focus is on grouping information into categories.	Words such as *can be classified, are grouped, there are two types*	To identify topics, list class or group factors, understand how they differ, and classify new information.	Identify and restate the general topic. Write down the categories and related information in a table with columns.

McGee and Richgels (1985) recommended a seven-step procedure for providing explicit instruction in any one of a number of specific text structures:

1. Select a textbook passage that is a good example of the structure you want to teach.
2. Prepare a graphic organizer showing key ideas and how they are related (the structure).

3. Introduce students to the text structure and show them the organizer.
4. Have students use the information in the organizer to write a passage.
5. Encourage them to use key words to show the relationships among ideas.
6. Have them read the textbook passage and compare what they wrote with the actual passage.
7. Help students visualize patterns and the ways ideas are connected (Irwin, 1991).

Compare–Contrast Strategy

Williams (2005) taught students how to use (1) clue words to identify a text as a compare–contrast text, (2) a graphic organizer to lay out the relevant information in the text, and (3) a series of questions to help them focus on the important. The first lesson focused on cats and dogs (familiar content) to introduce students to the program.

Lessons included:

1. *Clue words*: *alike, both, and, compare, but, however, then,* and *contrast*. The teacher introduces the words and also previews the purpose of the lesson.
2. *Trade book reading and discussion*: The teacher reads to the class from the encyclopedia and trade books and then leads a discussion about the content. The teacher provides information about the topic beyond the specific information contained in the target paragraphs. The purpose is to increase motivation, given that students' ability to comprehend expository text is based, in part, on their interest (Armbruster et al., 1987).
3. *Vocabulary development*: The teacher introduces vocabulary related to topic.
4. *Reading and analysis of a target paragraph*: Students read the target paragraph silently, and then the teacher rereads it aloud while students follow along. Students then analyze the text, using the compare–contrast structure. They identify the individual sentences that represent specific similarities and differences and circle key words. Then they take turns generating sentences that describe similarities and differences. The teacher models how to do this and encourages well-formed sentences based on information from the paragraph and including at least one clue word.
5. *Graphic organizer*: Students organize the paragraph's content with the help of a compare–contrast matrix (one for each feature compared). Students write a well-structured comparative statement to match the content in the matrix.
6. *Compare–contrast strategy questions*: Students organize the statements they have generated using these three questions: (a) What two things is this paragraph about? (b) How are those two things the same? (c) How are they different?

7. *Summary (with a paragraph frame as support)*: Students write summaries, using a paragraph frame as a prompt. This step is particularly helpful with younger students, as in this study, who are just starting to develop their writing skills (Harris & Graham, 1999). In later lessons, when students are more proficient, no frame is needed.

8. *Lesson review*: The teacher and students review the vocabulary and strategies (clue words, graphic organizer, and compare–contrast questions).

Dickson et al. (1995) also promoted an approach for helping students identify the compare–contrast text structure and using it to facilitate their comprehension. Their strategy focused on the similarities and differences between topics signaled by words such as *like, different, in contrast*, and *but*. Dickson (1999) found that the compare–contrast structure could be taught successfully in middle school inclusive general education classrooms. The following steps can help students identify this structure:

1. Identify two topics being compared and contrasted.
2. Look for key compare–contrast words such as *alike, different, but*.
3. Determine the organization of the compare–contrast structure. This organization can be:
   a. Whole–whole, where the author(s) describe each topic separately, with a different paragraph or set of paragraphs for each.
   b. Part–part, where the author(s) present a feature-by-feature comparison of two topics.
   c. Mixed, where the author(s) might first discuss each topic separately and then provide a feature-by-feature analysis in another paragraph.
4. Locate the explanation of how the topics are the same.
5. Locate the explanation of how the topics are different.

See Figure 4.6 for a Compare–Contrast Think-Sheet that can be used to help with reading comprehension or to plan for writing (Englert et al., 1995).

These next three models do not focus exclusively on text structures but are included in this chapter because they do address the organization of the text and the relationships among ideas.

Multipass

With the Multipass strategy, students make three "passes" through an expository text passage (Schumaker, Deshler, Alley, Warner, & Denton, 1984). The purpose is to help them find and remember key information in the passage.

1. During the first pass, called "Survey," students spend about 3 minutes skimming the text to become familiar with its main ideas and organization.

What two things are compared and contrasted?	

On what feature?	

Alike?	Different?

On what feature?	

Alike?	Different?

On what feature?	

Alike?	Different?

FIGURE 4.6. Compare–Contrast Think-Sheet. From Haager and Klingner (2005). Copyright 2005 by Pearson Education. Reprinted by permission.

They paraphrase the title of the chapter, note how the chapter relates to other chapters and the unit of study, and scan the chapter's introduction, headings, and summary.

2. During the next pass, called "Sort-out," they look for specific information in the text. They can do this by reading the questions at the end of the chapter and guessing at the answers, or they might turn each section heading into a question and skim the section to find the answer. Students also make study cards for key terms highlighted in the text.

3. During the last pass, called "Size-up," they read the text to find the correct answers to the questions from the previous step. They also test themselves with the study cards they made earlier.

Teachers teach students how to use the Multipass strategy by explaining and modeling each of these three steps. Students then take turns verbally rehearsing each step until they can perform it correctly without prompts. They then practice the strategy with a text at their reading level, with feedback from the instructor. As students become more proficient using Multipass, they should try it with more difficult texts. The teacher evaluates students on each step of Multipass and checks their understanding of the text with a comprehension test at the end of each completed chapter.

Hierarchical Summary Procedure

Taylor (1982) suggested this technique for use with middle school students to direct their attention to the organizational structure of passages. The procedure has five steps:

1. *Previewing*: Students preview a few pages of the text and generate an outline of numbers and letters for the sections indicated in the text.
2. *Reading*: Students read, filling in the sections.
3. *Outlining*: For each section, students write a main idea in their own words; they summarize the subsection into key phrases.
4. *Studying*: After they have finished reading, students review their summaries.
5. *Retelling*: Students orally retell what they learned, with a partner.

Interactive Instructional Model

Bos and Anders (1992) developed the interactive instructional model to enhance the text comprehension and content-area learning of students with LD. This model relies on semantic feature analysis and uses relationship maps (see Chapter 3), relationship charts, and interactive strategic dialogues. The steps of the interactive instructional model are as follows:

1. Before reading, students make a *brainstorm list* of what they already know about the topic.
2. They make a *clue list* using what the text indicates about the topic.
3. They make a *relationship map* or *relationship chart* to predict how the concepts are related.
4. They *read* to confirm their understanding and to integrate the relationships among concepts.
5. After reading, they *review* and *revise* their map or chart.
6. They use the map or chart to *study* for a test or *write* about what they learned.

Students apply these steps while working together in cooperative groups. As students become increasingly proficient at implementing the steps in the model and supporting one other, the role of the teacher changes to that of a facilitator (Bos & Anders, 1992).

CONCLUSION

Although students with LD are often unaware of, or confused by, different text structures, the good news is that explicit instruction can help them recognize these various structures and use that recognition to aid their comprehension. This finding seems to be true for students at different grade levels, from the primary grades through high school. However, as Williams (2005) noted, even when text structure strategies are found to be successful with most students, we cannot assume that every child exposed to the model or strategy will improve. Thus, it is important to try different approaches to achieve maximal benefit for the most students possible.

TEXT STRUCTURE SAMPLE LESSON PLANS
(to Accompany Chapter 4)

PICTURE STORIES

Grade Levels

Early elementary and learners who struggle with story recall

Purpose

To understand that stories follow a logical sequence.

Materials

Index cards
Colored pencils, markers

Lesson

1. *Identify that your day has a beginning, a middle, and an end.*

- Discuss the sequence of the day: waking up, getting dressed, eating breakfast, going to school, etc.
- Tell students that they will write a "My-Day" picture story of their day.
- Give students five index cards; on each card students should draw something they do during the day.
- Students then arrange the cards in order, from the first thing they do to the last. Talk about how the day would not make sense if the events were out of order.
- Students can tell their stories to a partner or the class. Connect the cards in order and display in class. Point out that each student's day follows a sequential order, even if events are different.
- Connect the sequence to a sequential text structure.

2. *Extend the lesson.*

- Students use the sequenced pictures to write the story of their day.
- Students create a picture story to retell a story they read or one that was read to them.
- Students create a picture story of a more complex sequencing activity, such as baking a cake or learning how to ride a bike.

Adaptation for Students with Special Needs

- This activity is especially useful for students who do not readily recognize how stories are organized. Applying the sequencing text structure to events that occur in one's own life makes the text structure more explicit.
- If students have trouble accurately retelling a story, even when they create a picture story for retelling, refer to their "My-Day" picture stories to cue them to sequence the events in order. Comments such as the following provide helpful cues for students who do not sequence easily: "Remember in your picture story that you got dressed before you went to school. Your day wouldn't make sense if everything was out of order. Try to tell what happened in the story we just read by putting the events in order. What happened to Ralph Mouse before he decided to live at school?"
- Sometimes students become so focused on recalling events in order that their comprehension decreases. After reading a story, have students write, dictate, or draw five things that happened in it. Allow them to freely remember events from the story. Once they have written or drawn their events, cut the sentences or pictures apart and have students assemble them in order. Add other important information or details that are needed to create an accurate retell of the story. Later, students can move on to writing/drawing/dictating the events in a story in order.
- Some students get caught up in interesting details, making it difficult for them to summarize just the most important information. The following variation assists students in identifying the most important information in a story: Repeat the activity above but then have students select only the most important ideas or events from the events they remembered. Add information as needed so that the retold story contains only the key ideas.

UNCOVER THE TEXT STRUCTURE

Grade Levels

Upper elementary through high school

Purpose

To identify expository text structures found in content-area textbooks.

Materials

Text structure cue cards
Content-area textbook

Lesson

It can be difficult to identify and distinguish between different text structures. Therefore, teaching text structure requires a series of lessons that are scaffolded to encourage student learning and transfer. We recommend the following steps over a series of lessons:

1. Provide explicit instruction in one type of text structure at a time, with opportunities for student feedback and practice.
2. As you introduce the second text structure, compare it to the one that has been previously learned. Initially, it is helpful to limit comparisons to two text structure types at a time (e.g., description and sequence).
3. Finally, students can be expected to identify the text structure of readings in expository text as they read for meaning during lessons.

1. *Explicitly teach text structure.*

- Use a short passage that is a good example of the text structure you wish to teach. For example, you may wish to start with the descriptive text type.
- Read the passage aloud to students and use the cue card to model how you decide which text structure type it is. Descriptive text structure cue card: Describes the attributes, specifics, and/or setting. The main idea is the "who, what, where, when, why, and how." Describe how some of the signal words and phrases help you determine the text structure.
- Give students another passage to read of the same text type and ask them to explain why it is a descriptive text structure. This practice will help students internalize the definition of the specific text type and provide practice they will need to distinguish between text types later on.

2. *Introduce a second text structure type.*

- The next day, review the first text type with another short passage. Ask students to provide a rationale. They should become more familiar with the definition and be able to explain their reasoning.
- Now, introduce a second text type in the same manor; first, by repeating the steps above, and then by contrasting the two text types.

3. *Once students are familiar with text structure, have them identify the text structure after reading.*

- Continue to provide feedback and to make connections between a reading's text structure (e.g., comparison) and the information and understanding that are associated with each.
- If students are unable to identify text structure, provide additional instruction as needed.

Adaptation for Students with Special Needs

Whereas some students catch on quickly to text structure forms, others may have difficulty. Many students who struggle to apply new concepts have not learned them adequately to begin with (Bransford, Brown, & Cocking, 1999). If a student is not able to apply a specific text structure to reading passages, or if he or she cannot distinguish between text structure types, ask the following questions and reteach or provide additional practice as needed.

- Can the student identify the text structure with a practice passage? If not:
  - Use other passages and provide additional direct instruction.
  - Provide a context or examples of when this text structure is typically used.
  - "Think aloud" while creating a passage of the text type, highlighting the features and signal words that would be present.
  - Model how to use the cue cards to figure out the text structure.
  - Ask the student to create a passage using the text structure.
- Can the student provide the rationale for the specific text structure? For example, "I know this is a problem–solution text type because Christopher Columbus wanted to find a shorter route to Asia, and he asked the king to give him a boat and crew so he could find a shorter way to get there to solve his problem." If not:
  - Supply more practice passages and have the struggling student work with a student who is familiar with text structures. At first, the partner can provide the rationale, and the struggling student can restate. Later, the struggling student can provide the rationale, and the partner can give feedback.
- Can the student distinguish between two text structure types? If not:
  - Repeat the suggestions above and then provide more practice with distinguishing between two text types.
  - Provide sample passage and offer two cue cards for the student to choose between. Be sure that the student uses the cue cards to provide a rationale for why he or she has chosen one text structure type over another.
- Can the student identify text structure in reading passages after explicit instruction and practice have been successfully completed? If not:
  - Have the student use the cue cards systematically to determine which text structure is present, beginning with description and moving through to problem–solution.
  - Be sure that the text structure is clear. Occasionally, a passage will present more than one text structure (e.g., causation and problem–solution). If the student can provide an acceptable rationale, he or she is showing mastery.
  - Check for understanding. If the student is able to understand and remember the important information, identifying text structure may not be an essential strategy for this particular student.

CHAPTER 5

Instructional Practices That Promote Reading Comprehension

STUDY GROUP PROMPTS

1. Before reading this chapter, discuss the comprehension strategies that you use in your classroom before, during, and after reading. Are there strategies that have been especially beneficial for students who struggle to understand and remember what they read? Are there strategies that are not as effective as you would like them to be?

2. As you read the chapter, make note of strategies that you might like to implement. How are these strategies similar to, or different from, practices you are currently using?

3. After reading, review individual lists and select one new strategy that you and another colleague will implement. Create a plan that includes how you will (a) integrate the strategy into your reading program, (b) introduce it to your students, and (c) monitor student progress. Be sure to schedule times to check in and share ideas.

4. After reading, discuss the ways in which you currently teach new strategies to your students in any subject area. How can you build on your experience to plan effective implementation of strategies suggested in this chapter?

This chapter focuses on effective ways to teach students to use comprehension strategies before, during, and after reading to assist them in understanding and remembering what they read. Most of the time, mature readers monitor comprehension unconsciously or at least so seamlessly that they are not always aware that they are using self-thinking, questioning, and monitoring, which are often referred to as metacognitive strategies. A good way for very experienced readers to check their comprehension strategies is by reading unfamiliar text. Consider the strategies you use while reading the following passage.

> In addition to reducing the concentration of bacteria and suspended particles in the treatment process, protozoa are also biotic indicators. The presence of protozoa reflects an improvement in effluent quality and is essential for the production of good quality effluent. (Lee, Basu, Tyler, & Wei, 2004, p. 371)

When we encounter difficult text, even good readers make explicit use of strategies. How did you approach this passage? Did you find yourself rereading elements of the text? Did you wonder about the meaning of some of the vocabulary words, such as *effluent* and *biotic*? Our guess is that most of us without a science background would have found it useful to link our understanding of similar topics to information in this passage. If this topic were unfamiliar, it might help to know that the key idea of this paragraph, and those that follow, is that microorganisms present in wastewater treatment plants are responsible for water quality. Also, we often talk about how important it is to have a "purpose" for reading. Would you have benefited from a purpose for reading this text? Reading unfamiliar text with unknown words or ideas is facilitated when the reader is armed with effective reading strategies and opportunities to ask questions and interact with others about what he or she has read. In this chapter we review what we know about reading comprehension instruction and what teachers can do to successfully improve the reading comprehension of their students with LD and other students who struggle to make sense of what they read.

INSTRUCTIONAL PRACTICES IN READING COMPREHENSION FOR STUDENTS WITH LEARNING DISABILITIES

What instructional practices can teachers use to improve the reading comprehension of struggling readers? First consider the skills identified in Chapter 1 that are associated with improved reading comprehension: word study, fluency, vocabulary, and world knowledge. Reading comprehension is supported by integrating a variety of instructional practices into your teaching routines, including the reading comprehension strategies and skills presented in this chapter.

There are several valuable sources of background knowledge on effective instruction in reading comprehension. One source is the National Reading Panel report (National Institute of Child Health and Human Development, 2000), which synthesizes reading comprehension intervention strategies. Though not specific to students with reading and learning disabilities, the panel was able to identify intervention practices, based on 203 studies, associated with improved outcomes in reading comprehension. These include:

- Teaching students to monitor their comprehension and to implement procedures when difficulties in understanding text arise.
- Using cooperative learning practices while implementing comprehension strategies in the context of reading.
- Providing graphic and semantic organizers that assist students in writing about, or drawing, relationships from the story.
- Providing support for questioning strategies through (1) story structures that assist students in answering critical questions about the passage, (2) feedback to students regarding their answers to questions about the text, and (3) opportunities for students to ask and answer their own questions about the text.
- Teaching students to write important ideas about what they've read and to summarize these ideas after longer passages are read.
- Teaching students to use multicomponent strategies that integrate and apply several strategies.

This chapter presents strategies, skills, and practices that have demonstrated effectiveness in improving reading comprehension. Multicomponent strategies for integrating several skills are described in Chapter 6.

BEFORE READING

What can teachers do prior to reading of text to enhance reading comprehension for students with significant reading comprehension difficulties? One of the most effective practices relates to schema theory (presented in Chapter 1). Accessing appropriate schema influences both understanding and memory. Teachers who spend even a few minutes linking students' background knowledge—that is, activating schema—to the text they are about to read improve their students' understanding of that text (Palincsar & Brown, 1984; Paris & Oka, 1986; Pressley, 2000). For students who are familiar with the content of a passage, linking related background knowledge, to text is easy. On the other hand, poor readers may have limited prior knowledge or they may fail to make connections between what they know and what they are learning. Indeed, prior knowledge can even interfere with comprehension when readers attempt to make connections and inferences using information that is not relevant to the most important ideas in the text (Williams, 1993). Therefore, it is important for teachers to create a context for students that facilitates comprehension by identifying key concepts, ideas, and words and then to preteach them, especially when reading expository text (Readence, Bean, & Baldwin, 1998). This introduction to the text provides enough background for many students to prepare them for reading and learning from what they read.

Successfully bridging what students know or need to know to what they are learning is essential. Graves, Calfee, Graves, and Juel (2006) and Graves, Juel, and Graves (2001) suggest the following activities prior to reading:

- Set a purpose for reading.
- Motivate students to read.
- Preteach key vocabulary and concepts.
- Link students' background knowledge and experiences with the reading.
- Relate the reading to students' lives (making connections).
- Build students' knowledge of the text features.

Setting a Purpose

Reading is an activity that has a purpose. When you want to know how to change a flat tire on your bicycle, you pick up a bicycle maintenance manual and flip to the section on tires. If you are researching the history of the computer, you would select a book that outlines the progression of computer use and its influence on society over time. If you are interested in adventure travels, you might look for a book about a person who toured the world in a hot air balloon. Whether you are reading for enjoyment, to gain factual or procedural knowledge, or to learn skills such as how to analyze poetry, being aware of the purpose for reading is an essential first step.

Whereas good readers easily determine why they are reading a specific text, readers who struggle may need help in setting the purpose for reading. Blanton and colleagues suggest that for struggling readers, it is best to set one purpose for reading, as opposed to multiple purposes (Blanton, Wood, & Moorman, 1990). Furthermore, the purpose should be broad enough to apply to an entire reading selection. Cunningham and Wall (1994) also suggest providing students with a goal for reading or a guide to the task in which they will be asked to engage after reading. For example, prior to using a microscope for the first time, a teacher might want students to build background knowledge of what a microscope is and how it is used. A teacher might say:

"Today we will be using a microscope for the first time. To introduce you to why microscopes are used, we will read about the history of the microscope and how it can be used in science laboratories."

This short introduction to the reading guides students to read efficiently. They will not be asked to memorize or critique the text but to acquire background knowledge that will prepare them for the activity of using a microscope to analyze scientific specimens. In most cases, setting the purpose for reading involves simply stating *why* students are reading the selection.

Text Preview

Text preview is a technique that motivates students to read for understanding by providing a structure with which they can integrate prior knowledge with the text (Graves, Prenn, & Cooke, 1985; Graves et al., 2001). At the end of this chapter we provide a lesson plan that shows how to preview text with students. Following are a few procedures for text previewing that we have found especially useful.

Teacher-Presented Text Preview

This previewing method is prepared and presented by the teacher, who provides an organizational framework that assists students in bridging their experiences to the reading by (1) cuing them to the new reading, (2) discussing an interesting part of the story, and (3) connecting the text to students' experiences and knowledge and presenting questions to guide the reading. Next, we describe the three steps involved in text preview with examples that relate to an expository reading on smoking from a kids weekly news magazine (Lorio, 2006):

1. Read a short selection from the text or provide interesting information about the reading that piques students' interest. For example, "Did you know that, every day, about 4,000 kids try smoking for the first time?"
2. Give a brief description of the theme or story organization. For example, "This reading is about the prevalence of smoking and how a group of kids has started a successful anti-smoking campaign in their community."
3. Ask questions to guide reading. For example, "What are some of the ways that kids have gotten their voices heard about the dangers of smoking?"

Interactive Text Preview

Another format for previewing text is interactive. Whereas the teacher still leads the preview, this form involves discussion and input from students. One strategy is to create a K-W-L (know, want to know, learn) chart (Ogle, 1986, 1989). A K-W-L chart can be done as a whole group, small group, partners, or as an individual activity. There are several versions of this activity; here we provide a popular version below:

1. Give each student a copy of the reading material and the K-W-L chart.
2. Before reading, teach students to preview the passage by looking at such features as headings and subheadings, pictures and captions, and words in bold or highlighted print.
3. Students then use a chart (either individual or whole group) to record "What I already know" about this topic in the first column of the chart and "What I want to learn" in the second column (see Figure 5.1).
4. During reading, students write in the third column of the K-W-L chart, "What I know"—what they learned in the text related to what they already knew or wanted to learn.
5. After reading, revisit the chart as a wrap-up to reading. Lead students in a discussion in which they review what they already knew, how it was addressed in the reading, what they learned that was new, and what they still need to confirm or learn more about.

A confirmation guide is a variation on the traditional K-W-L chart (Texas Education Agency, 2001; see Figure 5.2). The purpose of the confirmation guide is to

Name:		
Topic:		
K-W-L		
What I already *know*	What I *want* to learn	What I *learned*

FIGURE 5.1. K-W-L chart. Adapted from Ogle (1986, 1989). Copyright 1986, 1989 by The International Reading Association. Adapted by permission.

assist students in making explicit connections between prior knowledge and what they read. Similar to the K-W-L chart, students first preview the text and then write what they already know about the topic. The purpose of previewing the text prior to writing what they know about a topic is to assist students in grounding their prior knowledge in the specific text they will be reading. For example, during a general brainstorming session on whales, students are likely to provide a wide array of relevant and irrelevant information. However, after previewing a reading on endangered humpback whales, teachers can guide students to connect what they already know *as it relates to* endangered species and humpback whales. During reading, students provide information that confirms or rejects their prior knowledge statements. They provide "proof" of this information by including the

Name(s):		
Topic:		
Confirmation Guide		
What I already know	What I learned	Pages

FIGURE 5.2. Confirmation guide. Adapted from Texas Education Agency (2001) and University of Texas Center for Reading and Language Arts (2001). Copyright 2001 by Texas Education Agency. Adapted by permission.

page number where they read the information. Again, after reading, teachers lead a discussion of what was learned in the reading, how it connects to prior knowledge, and how the new information adds to, or changes, previous understandings about the topic.

Concept or semantic maps (presented in Chapter 4) are also appropriate previewing activities. These visual representations are used to present key ideas and vocabulary and to make connections to previously learned material. One such strategy includes the following steps:

1. Tell students the theme or big idea of the text and identify key concepts or vocabulary. Write the big idea in the middle circle on an overhead or chalkboard.
2. Ask students to connect the big idea to what they already know about the topic. Organize big idea and prior knowledge statements given by students and draw connecting lines between them.
3. Use the concept map to identify and briefly address misconceptions; clarify ideas and connections.
4. Ask students to make predictions about what they will learn by looking at the title, headings, and pictures of the reading.

Although previewing activities are common among teachers, it may be helpful to consider the following guidelines:

- Prepare and lead previewing. In most cases, even when students collaborate in discussions, it is appropriate for teachers to direct the previewing activities. The teacher (1) provides links or facilitates student-provided connections that activate background knowledge, (2) intersperses "hooks" that motivate students, and (3) identifies key ideas and vocabulary.
- Keep it short. Don't let previewing activities go on too long; 5–10 minutes is usually sufficient.
- Revisit the previewing activity after reading to assist in reviewing, summarizing, and making connections.

A few well-planned minutes of providing a purpose for reading, previewing, and building background knowledge will yield dividends in students' comprehension (Chen & Graves, 1995; Dole, Valencia, Greer, & Wardrop, 1991).

DURING AND AFTER READING

The most important strategies for students to implement while they are reading are those that assist them in monitoring their understanding (National Institute of Child Health and Human Development, 2000). All of us can remember times when we were reading and turning the pages, but we were not monitoring what we were reading. All of a sudden we looked down and noticed that we were several pages past when we last remembered what we were reading. In other instances, as in the example of expository text at the beginning of this chapter, the text is very dense and difficult, and we do not readily comprehend as we read. What do we do? Most of us go back and reread quickly and try to repair what we missed. Sometimes we seek assistance by getting more background information or finding the meaning of unfamiliar words or concepts. Other times we look forward in the reading to find explanatory information.

What can teachers do to assure that students monitor their comprehension? Most students with LD need to learn the same fix-up strategies that mature readers use to (1) identify when understanding breaks down and (2) know how to repair what they missed. These strategies can be taught to students (Pressley, 2000). Teachers can assist students in using comprehension strategies by doing the following:

- Encourage students to monitor their understanding while they read and to make notes of difficult words, concepts, or ideas.
- Ask students questions during reading to guide and focus their reading.
- Focus students on aspects of the text that require inferences.
- Ask students to summarize the main idea of passages as they read.
- Remind students to consider predictions made prior to reading and confirm, disconfirm, or extend them.
- Give students opportunities to respond to, and elaborate on, what they've read.
- Allow students to formulate questions about what they've read and then to answer those questions.
- Ask students to summarize the key ideas about their reading.

Perhaps one of the most important activities related to improving reading comprehension concerns what students do after they read. Students benefit from summarizing the key ideas they've read and responding to the reading in various ways, including writing, drawing, and discussing. After reading, students can identify concepts or words that were difficult and seek clarification. The most effective strategies for students with reading problems to learn to apply both during and after reading are (1) questioning and (2) formulating main idea and summarizing. Instructional practices for teaching each of these strategies are discussed separately.

Questioning

One of the teacher's more challenging jobs is to ask questions that engage students in thinking about what they've read. Teachers view questions as a means of determining whether students truly understand and make connections with text. Smart questioning is an essential feature of assessing reading comprehension and a tool for extending understanding of what was read. On the other hand, many questions teachers ask can limit responses and critical thinking. Asking good questions that engage and involve students to promote understanding is a skill. Although questioning occurs before, during, and after reading, some of the most important questioning occurs after reading. Next we offer strategies for making the most of teacher and student questions.

Teacher-Initiated Questions

In a classic study of teacher questioning, Susskind (1979) observed that teachers in grades 3–6 asked an average of about 50 questions in a 30-minute period. In that same time, students asked fewer than two questions. Furthermore, teachers typically wait less than 2 seconds for a student response and even less time for students who are perceived to be low achieving (Stahl, 1994). Students benefit when you provide them with just a little bit more "wait time" before moving on to another student or answering your own question! By increasing silent wait time to just 3 seconds, the following benefits are likely to occur (Rowe, 1986; Stahl, 1994):

- Students' responses are longer and more accurate.
- The number of "I don't know" and no-answer responses decreases.
- Correct responses by a larger proportion of the class increase.
- The number of teacher-initiated questions decreases, but the quality and variety of question types increases.

There are many factors that go into asking effective questions. The type of questions should relate to the content and skills that are being taught. Whereas some questions promote short, factual answers, others encourage discussion and evaluation of the material. Teachers who identify *why* they are asking questions and what outcomes they are expecting from students ask questions that yield better responses. Figure 5.3 provides suggestions to help teachers ask thoughtful questions that promote student understanding.

Often, teachers overlook the skills it takes for students to answer their questions. In general education classrooms, low-achieving students and students with disabilities are not only asked fewer questions than their normally achieving peers, they also answer far fewer questions (McIntosh, Vaughn, Schumm, Haager, & Lee, 1993). Teaching students how to answer teacher-initiated questions prepares them to benefit from discussions about reading. Teaching the following procedure assists students in organizing the process of answering teacher-initiated questions (Gall, 1984; Walsh & Sattes, 2005). Teachers can provide students with a question cue card to guide how they answer questions. For example, for a student who tends to blurt out answers without thinking first, you can cue him or her to respond more thoughtfully by referring to the steps on the following question cue card:

1. Listen to the question.
2. Figure out what you are being asked.

Determine content focus:
- Identify important facts, skills, and content.
- Establish if all students are responsible for learning all content (i.e., answering all questions).

Identify the purpose of the question:
- Consider classroom goals and skills. For example, question can be designed to motivate and engage students, check for understanding, review for a test, cue students to important content, reinforce knowledge, formulate and listen to new points of view, allow students to transfer learning to other situations.
- Develop questions specific to comprehension features. Questions can inquire about such features as main idea, sequence, setting, plot, details, vocabulary, inference, evaluation, or creative response.

Select question level:
- Ask a variety of question types. Questions can require factual responses, making connections, analyzing, creating, evaluating, or applying.
- Be sure that students have the skills to answer the questions. If not, teach those skills.

Encourage in-depth responses:
- Require students to support their opinions with information from the text.
- Individualize questions according to student needs. For example, one student can answer "How did the child feel when her grandmother arrived?" whereas another child might need the following question that provides more information, "Why did the child feel angry when her grandmother arrived?"
- Use specific terms to guide students to answer questions. For example, ask them to predict, compare or contrast, or infer.

Consider question wording:
- Ask questions that are clear and not too long. Students can only answer questions that they understand. Don't ask multiple questions within a question.

FIGURE 5.3. Preparing effective questions. Adapted from Walsh and Sattes (2005). Copyright 2005 by Corwin Press. Adapted by permission.

3. Answer to yourself.
4. Answer out loud.
5. If needed, rethink and try again.

In another strategy that assists students who struggle to answer teacher-generated or end-of-chapter-type questions, the teacher provides explicit instruction in identifying and differentiating between various question types (Blachowicz & Ogle, 2001; Bos & Vaughn, 2002; National Institute of Child Health and Human Development, 2000; Raphael, 1986). Raphael (1986) came up with question–answer relationships (QARs) to teach students strategies with which to answer different question types. Students learn to categorize questions by the type of information that is used to answer them. In the technique described below, specific QARs are taught and practiced by students. Students can use the following QAR question types to analyze and answer teacher-initiated questions or to create their own questions:

1. *Right There*: Answers to these literal questions can be found in one sentence in the text. For example: "When was George Washington born?"

2. *Think and Search*: To find the answer to this type of question, students must draw conclusions, which requires that they integrate information from more than one place in the reading. Because these questions are more complex, they often require a sentence or more to answer. For example: "What factors might influence global warming?"

3. *The Author and You*: These questions require students to connect information from the text to what they have already learned and may require students to consider their own experiences and opinions or to extend what they have learned. For this question type, students are told that some of the information needed to answer the question comes from the text, but other information comes from things you already know. For example: "What would you have done if you were in Simone's position? How are the Comanche similar to other Native American tribes we have studied?"

4. *On Your Own*: These questions can be answered from the reader's own experience without information from the text. Many questions asked before reading that elicit students' prior knowledge are On Your Own questions. For extension activities after reading, teachers tend to ask On Your Own or Author and You question types to connect what students already know to what they have just read. For example: (Before reading) "What have you learned so far about mitosis?" (After reading) "Now that we have read about how global warming effects the seasons, how might global warming influence our own community?"

Many teachers have difficulty delineating between Author and You and On Your Own question types. The purpose of distinguishing between the two is to clarify that some questions are based primarily on background knowledge and can be answered sufficiently without reading the text. Other questions can be answered without reading the text, but we would expect more informed responses after reading. For example, the question above about global warming is an On Your Own question because it can be answered without reading the text. However, once students have read the text specific to global warming and the seasons, they should be able to provide more in-depth responses that use information from the reading to support their ideas. Indeed, this question could fall under either the On Your Own or Author and You categories. Some teachers decide to combine the last two question types.

Most students find it useful to use question cue cards to assist them in analyzing questions using QAR types. Each cue card has the question type, a brief definition, and an example. Figure 5.4 provides an example of a Think and Search question cue card.

"Think and Search"
☐ Questions can be answered by looking in the story.
☐ Answers are more complex; answers are one sentence or more.
☐ Answers are found in more than one place and put together. You must combine information that is located in different sentences, paragraphs, or pages of the story.
Example:
☐ To answer *What factors influenced the migration of the penguins?* several sentences are needed to describe the factors that are presented on different pages of the text.

FIGURE 5.4. Example of a *Think and Search* question cue card. Adapted from Texas Education Agency (2001) and University of Texas Center for Reading and Language Arts (2001). Copyright 2001 by Texas Education Agency. Adapted by permission.

Student-Generated Questions

Up to this point we have focused on teacher-initiated questions. Teachers who design questions that require students to draw conclusions, apply what they have learned, analyze what they have read, and synthesize and evaluate text advance student understanding and knowledge of reading. However, regardless of how interesting the question is, students are limited to answering the question posed by the teacher—a relatively passive activity (Kamil, 2004). Therefore, it is important not only for teachers to ask good questions, but also to teach and provide time for *students* to ask and answer their own questions (National Institute of Child Health and Human Development, 2000). Generating questions helps students engage with the text, monitor their understanding, remember what they've read, and connect what they are learning to what they already know. One technique that is very effective is to teach students to use the QAR question types described earlier to generate questions after reading. For example, after reading, students can create one question of each QAR type about what they read. To reinforce what they learned while reading, students then ask each other their questions.

An essential component of student questioning is the provision of direct instruction, support, and feedback to students as they learn how to ask and answer questions. Students who are familiar with QARs still need to learn how to generate questions, and you can adjust modeling and practice based on their experience. If students are not familiar with the question types, provide instruction on them and on how to generate questions at the same time. To do this, teach the question type by describing what the question is and thinking aloud how to create and answer the question. For example, when introducing Right There questions, you might say something such as:

> "Today we are going to learn about the first type of question. We call this a Right There question because the information needed to answer a Right There question can be found in one place in the reading selection. Answering

Right There questions is usually easy and requires little thinking or effort. Look at the passage we just read about George Washington. I can see here that it says 'George Washington was born on February 2, 1732.' That looks like a Right There answer because it's a fact and it's all in one sentence. My question is, 'When was George Washington born?' The answer is right there in the sentence."

Then allow students to practice, as you monitor and provide feedback. When students have a clear understanding of what a Right There question is, it prepares them to write their own questions. Once students are comfortable with the question types and how to create them, they can apply their skills by working together in pairs or small groups to ask and answer questions using the following procedures:

1. Students read the selected passage as determined by the teacher (e.g., choral reading, taking turns, one partner reads while the other follows along).
2. Each group member generates at least three questions from the reading.
3. Each student presents his or her questions to the partner or small-group members and gives feedback.

You can modify question asking for students with disabilities by telling students what kinds of questions to create. For example, a student who is still struggling with basic understanding might be asked to generate and answer three Right There questions, whereas other students might be asked to generate and answer one question of each type. Further, students who have difficulty generating questions can work at their own level but still answer a variety of questions generated by other students.

The same procedure can be used for generating the more familiar question types (i.e., the 5 Ws and an H: who, what, when, where, why, and how). For these questions, students first learn to generate the "who, what, when, and where" questions and then move on to "why and how" questions.

For factually dense material such as some social studies and science texts, teaching students to ask themselves "why" questions as they read is especially effective. As students read, they are taught to continually ask themselves why the facts make sense. In a study of fourth- to eighth-grade science classrooms, students asked themselves why facts made sense (e.g., Why do skunks eat corn? Why do owls prey on skunks?) and then attempted to answer the "why" questions using prior knowledge (Pressley, Schuder, SAIL, Bergman, & El-Dinary, 1992; Wood, Pressley, & Winne, 1990). Students who learned to ask why questions remembered what they had read better than students who read the text without asking questions. This procedure is effective because it helps students connect relevant prior knowledge to what they are reading, and it makes the facts they are reading about more memorable.

Combining Teacher and Student Questions

An effective way for teachers to guide students in asking and answering worth-while questions about what they read is a questioning-the-author technique (see Table 5.1; Beck, McKeown, Sandora, Kucan, & Worthy, 1996). With this technique the teacher has distinct goals and several queries that assist students in reaching those goals. The idea of this technique is that students benefit when they think about why the author made the decisions he or she did and what questions or com-ments they would like to make to the author if they could meet him or her. For example, after reading *The Lorax* by Dr. Seuss, a student asked, "Why didn't Dr. Seuss draw a picture of The Onceler?" This question spurred a lively discussion among students and the teacher about why the author would choose to leave one of the main characters hidden from our view and how this choice influences how

TABLE 5.1. Queries Developed to Guide Discussions during Questioning the Author

Goal	Queries
Initiate discussion.	• What is the author trying to say? • What is the author's message? • What is the author talking about?
Help students focus on the author's message.	• That's what the author says, but what does it mean?
Help students link information.	• How does that connect with what the author already told us? • How does that fit in with what the author already told us? • What information has the author added here that connects to, or fits in with, _____?
Identify difficulties with the way the author has presented information or ideas.	• Does that make sense? • Is that said in a clear way? • Did the author explain that clearly? Why or why not? What's missing? What do we need to figure out or find out?
Encourage students to refer to the text either because they've misinterpreted a text statement or to help them recognize that they've made an inference.	• Did the author tell us that? • Did the author give us the answer to that?

Note. From Beck, McKeown, Sandora, Kucan, and Worthy (1996). Copyright 1996 by University of Chicago Press. Reprinted by permission.

we understand and interpret the story. According to McKeown and Beck (2004), "the development of meaning in this technique focuses on readers' interactions with text as it is being read, situates reader–text interactions in whole-class discussion, and encourages explanatory, evidence based responses to questions about text" (p. 393). Through their study of many classrooms, McKeown and Beck found that as teachers and students adopted this new stance to reading and questioning, patterns of discussion went from students providing pat answers to test-like questions to collaborative discussions that involved both teacher and students in questioning and the creation and elaboration of new ideas.

Another technique that combines high-quality teacher-initiated questions with student-generated ones is the ReQuest procedure (Manzo & Manzo, 1993), the steps to which follow:

1. *Silent reading.* The teacher and the student read the section of text independently and silently.
2. *Student questioning.* The teacher models how to answer questions and to shape student questions. Students ask questions and the teacher answers them.
3. *Teacher questioning.* The teacher models how to ask appropriate questions. Students answer questions and the teacher assists by shaping their responses.
4. *Integration of the text.* Repeat the procedure with the next section of text. This time integrate the previous section of text with the newly read section. Base questions and answers on both sections.
5. *Predictive questioning.* After students have read enough of the passage that they can make predictions about the rest of the text, stop and ask them to make predictions.
6. *Reading.* Read to the end of the text to verify predictions. Discuss changes.

Perhaps it seems like a big investment of time to teach questioning skills to students. Remember, there is strong evidence that teachers foster comprehension when they use effective questioning strategies and when they support students in asking and answering their own questions about reading passages. For more ideas about how to integrate effective questioning into reading comprehension instruction, see Chapter 6.

Formulating Main Ideas and Summarizing

Really understanding what we read can probably best be determined by how well and accurately we state a main idea and summarize our understanding. Although the terminology varies, there are generally two ways to think about these important skills. First, readers need to identify the central message or "gist" of small portions of text. We refer to this skill as finding the main idea. Second, readers must know how to synthesize larger amounts of text (e.g., several paragraphs, a page-long section, a chapter) into a summary that contains only the most important information.

Whether students are reading small or larger amounts of text,, they often erroneously do one or more of the following when asked to summarize what they have read:

- Write about everything.
- Write about selected details.
- Copy word for word.
- Don't write anything.

In contrast, when we teach students strategies to summarize after reading, they learn to do the following:

- Distinguish between important information and details.
- Use key vocabulary or concepts.
- Synthesize information.
- Use their own words.
- Write only what is needed to present the main idea(s).

Although we separate these strategies into main idea and summarization portions, you will see that many of the main idea skills can be extended to longer portions of text, and many of the summary strategies can also be pared down for paragraphs or short sections. In general, if students cannot determine the key ideas of what they have read once you have taught (and students have learned) a main idea or summarization strategy, then shorten the length of text.

Main Idea

Sometimes the main idea is stated explicitly (as in the topic sentence) and other times it is implicit and must be inferred. Knowing how to construct the main idea of what is read is essential because it helps students identify what is important to know and remember (Williams, 1988). Learning how to state or write a main idea may be even more important for students with LD because they rarely use comprehension strategies even when the difficulty level of the reading passage increases (Simmons, Kame'enui, & Darch, 1988). Fortunately, when students are taught how to explicitly and systematically identify the main idea, the result is improved outcomes in reading comprehension (Graves, 1986; Jenkins, Heliotis, Stein, & Haynes, 1987; Jitendra, Cole, Hoppes, & Wilson, 1998; Jitendra, Hoppes, & Xin, 2000; Wong & Jones, 1982). Also, direct instruction plus strategy instruction is the best combination for providing powerful interventions for students with LD (Swanson, 1999, 2001); thus, main idea instruction that includes both direct instruction and a strategy component is likely to yield the best outcomes.

The ability to find the main idea of a paragraph is a precursor to being able to summarize larger amounts of text. Although there are various ways to come up with the main idea, the skill involves identifying the subject of the paragraph and the most important ideas about the subject.

Jitendra et al. (2000) combined strategy and direct instruction to improve main idea use for students with LD. Students who learned this strategy significantly outperformed students who received reading instruction as usual, and their gains were maintained over time. In this study, middle school students were taught to use a main idea strategy in eight 30-minute lessons. The length of instruction is important to note because teaching reading comprehension strategies (or any learning strategies, for that matter) takes time. It is often the case that when students fail to apply a particular strategy it is because they have not learned it well initially (Bransford, Brown, & Cocking, 1999). In the technique reported by Jitendra and colleagues, the teacher goes through a series of steps to teach the skill of identifying the main idea:

1. *Present the main idea strategy.* First name the subject and then categorize the action.
2. *Model the application of the strategy with a reading passage.*
3. *Demonstrate the use of the self-monitoring cue card* (see Figure 5.5).
4. *Provide opportunities for guided and then independent practice using the main idea strategy with the self-monitoring cue card.* During this phase the teacher monitors performance and provides corrective feedback.

Paragraph Shrinking

Paragraph shrinking is a simple technique for identifying the main idea of a paragraph or short section of text. It is usually taught with reading strategies that are implemented using peer-assisted learning strategies (Fuchs, Fuchs, Mathes, & Simmons, 1997). The steps of paragraph shrinking are as follows:

Finding the Main Idea	
Does the paragraph tell:	
What or who the subject is?	Action is?
(Single or Group)	(Category)
Why—something happened?	
Where—something is or happened?	
When—something happened?	
How—something looks or is done?	
NOTE: Some paragraphs may contain a sentence or two that don't tell about the main idea!	

FIGURE 5.5. Main idea self-monitoring cue card. From Jitendra, Hoppes, and Xin (2000). Copyright 2000 by PRO-ED. Reprinted by permission.

1. Identify the subject of the paragraph by looking for the *who* or *what* the paragraph is mostly about.
2. State the most important information about the *who* or *what*.
3. Say the main idea in 10 or fewer words.

If you use peer tutors or partners, the tutor reads the paragraph, and then the student states the subject and main idea (although the roles may be switched). Working together in partners to read and process text increases engagement, active learning, and task persistence (e.g., Fuchs, Mathes, & Simmons, 1997).

Paraphrasing

Schumaker and colleagues (Schumaker, Denton, & Deshler, 1984) developed and evaluated the effectiveness of the paraphrasing strategy for use with expository or informational texts. First students read the paragraph and think about what it means while reading. Then they ask themselves to identify the main idea of the paragraph. Finally they put the main idea and supporting details into their own words. The acronym RAP is used to cue students to the steps in the strategy:

1. <u>R</u>ead a paragraph.
2. <u>A</u>sk yourself.
   - What are the main idea and details of this paragraph? If you're not sure, complete the following:
     - This paragraph is about _____.
     - It tells me about _____.
   - If you need more information:
     - Look in the first sentence of the paragraph.
     - Look for information that is repeated with the same word or words in more than one place.
     - Identify what the details describe or explain.
3. <u>P</u>ut the main idea and details into your own words.
   - Must be a complete sentence (subject and verb).
     - Must be accurate.
     - Must contain new information.
     - Must be in your own words.
     - Must contain only one general statement per paragraph.

Students first practice using the steps with a variety of informational sources such as textbooks, articles, and even teacher lectures. As students become more familiar with this strategy they learn not only why and how to apply it, but when it is the most useful (Berry, Hall, & Gildroy, 2004).

Cognitive Organizers

Cognitive organizers, which assist students in remembering and following learning strategy procedures, have been used effectively with main idea instruction. Cognitive organizers often employ mnemonic devices that cue students to the steps of the strategy. Although cognitive organizers can be used with students of all ages, they are frequently used with older students who can learn to use the steps independently. Boyle and Wishaar (1997) examined the effects of student-generated and expert-generated cognitive organizers (a cognitive organizer that has high utility, often developed by the teacher or textbook) on the reading comprehension of high school students with LD. Results indicated that the group that used student-generated cognitive organizers outperformed both the expert-generated and the control group on comprehension measures. The group that used student-generated organizers learned the following strategy steps (TRAVEL):

> <u>T</u>—Topic: Write down the topic.
> <u>R</u>—Read: Read the paragraph.
> <u>A</u>—Ask: Ask what the main idea and three details are and write them down.
> <u>V</u>—Verify: Verify the main idea and linking details.
> <u>E</u>—Examine: Examine the next paragraph and verify again.
> <u>L</u>—Link: When finished, link all of the main ideas.

Summarizing

Summarization requires students to generate multiple main ideas from across a reading and then to combine them to form a summary. In addition, students must be able to generalize from specific examples and be able to identify when information is repeated (National Institute of Child Health and Human Development, 2000). Learning to summarize is an effective strategy for improving comprehension for students with LD (Gajria & Salvia, 1992; Nelson, Smith, & Dodd, 1992). Many summarization strategies include rules that students learn to use to write summaries. Through modeling, feedback, and many opportunities to practice, students are taught to use the following rules (National Institute of Child Health and Human Development, 2000):

1. Delete trivial information.
2. Delete redundant information.
3. Use one word to replace a list of related items.
4. Select a topic sentence.
5. Invent a topic sentence if one is not explicitly stated.

Students are first taught to use the rules to write main idea statements for every paragraph. They are then taught to use the same rules to combine the information from their main idea statements to form a summary of main ideas. In other words, summarization is a hierarchical skill whereby readers gain experience first by finding the main idea of single paragraphs, then, once they have mastered the main idea skill, they learn to combine main ideas to form summary statements.

In another application of summarization, Jenkins and colleagues (Jenkins et al., 1987) improved performance on the retelling and recall of passages by students with LD by systematically teaching them to answer questions about what they read: (1) Who is it about? and (2) What's happening? Similarly, Malone and Mastropieri (1992) taught students to self-question while reading by asking (1) Who or what is the passage about? and (2) What is happening? Students with LD who participated in the training outperformed control students on recall of passage content.

Some students benefit from strategies that involve ways to cue recall of information visually. One way to do this is to use visual representations of the main ideas and supporting details for a reading selection (McCormick, 1999). Baumman (1984) combined instruction of summarization with this sort of visual representation with sixth-grade students. Results indicated that the strategy improved students' ability to conduct well-organized summaries. To use this strategy, students first generate main ideas of paragraphs or short sections as they read. After reading, the teacher leads a discussion using a picture to guide students' thinking. Each main idea statement is written onto the summary image. For example, in a text about ants, students are given a picture of an ant in which the body represents the topic statement and the legs represent the main ideas and supporting details. Once students are familiar with the strategy, they are given their own figure (or can create their own) and work together with a partner to complete representations of the main ideas and supporting details. When introducing the strategy or using it with younger students, visual representations can also be used to find the main idea of a paragraph. For example, students might first write details on the branches of a tree and then use the details to generate a main idea statement. Note that visual representations are more effective when used in combination with other summarization strategies, such as using the rules described above to combine main ideas.

Formulating main ideas and summarizations involves synthesizing a lot of information to come up with what a paragraph, section, or passage is mostly about. Summarization skills demonstrate a student's ability to articulate an understanding of what is read. It is also the area with which students who struggle with reading comprehension have the most difficulty. The main idea and summarization strategies presented in this section are examples of effective techniques that teachers can use to improve these essential skills.

Strategies for Understanding Narrative Text

The final section of this chapter focuses on strategies that are especially (although not exclusively) useful with narrative text.

Story Retelling

Story retelling is a strategy that involves recounting what has just been read in sequential order. Story retelling can be an effective practice for determining and assuring reading comprehension of narrative text (Bos, 1987). Retelling a story demonstrates a student's ability to identify the story's important events and also provides a purpose for continued reading.

You can first model the retelling strategy by identifying the key components of a story: character, setting, and problem and resolution. For students who struggle with these components, teaching them separately and then combining them can be an effective tool. For example:

Simple retelling
- Identify and retell the beginning, middle, and end of the story.
- Describe the setting.
- Identify the problem and resolution.

More complete retelling
- Identify and retell events and facts in a sequence.
- Make inferences to fill in missing information.
- Identify and retell causes of actions or events and their effects.

Most complete retelling
- Identify and retell a sequence of actions or events.
- Make inferences to account for events or actions.
- Offer an evaluation of the story.

Identifying Themes

Students with LD can learn to identify themes from stories and determine the extent to which those themes apply to their own lives (Williams, 1998). Identifying themes helps students feel personally connected to what they are reading and renders the information more relevant and thus more memorable. Text that contains a suitable theme (e.g., cooperation, responsibility, or respect for others) is identified and used as the source for the following lesson parts:

1. *Conduct a prereading discussion about lesson purpose and story topic.* The teacher identifies the theme and facilitates understanding initially, then scaffolds the use of this strategy with the goal of having students identify the story theme independently.

2. *Read the story.* The teacher now reads the story and stops to ask questions to ascertain whether students are connecting what they are reading to the story theme.

3. *Discuss important story information using organizing (schema) questions.* The following three questions are used to assist students in organizing the story information:

> Who is the main character?
> What did he or she do?
> What happened?

After students understand the organization of the story, they are asked the following questions to assist them in integrating the story information with the theme:

> Was this good or bad?
> Why was this good or bad?

4. *Identify the theme in a standard format.* Students learn to state the theme in a standard format by identifying what the character should or should not have done and then what they (the students) should or should not do.

5. *Apply the theme to real-life experiences.* In this section, the students are encouraged to consider to whom the theme applies and under what conditions.

Using Character Motives

In a variation on the above strategy, teachers use direct instruction to teach students to identify character motives. Being able to identify character motive is an important skill because to understand a text, the reader must remember a series of actions and then determine the motive for those actions (Shannon, Kame'enui, & Bauman, 1988). In this strategy, teachers incorporate rule statements, multistep procedures, and demonstration into the direct instruction model to teach character motive to students with disabilities. Consonant with direct instruction is the use of "rule-based instructional strategies." The direct instruction model has several specific features that were used by Rabren, Darch, and Eaves (1999) to help students learn to identify character motive. They are "(a) presentation of an explicit, problem-solving strategy, (b) mastery teaching of each step in the strategy, (c) development of specific correction procedures for student error, (d) a gradual transition from teacher-directed work to independent work, and (e) built-in cumulative review of previously taught concepts" (p. 89). Figure 5.6 provides the lesson structure used in this study. Darch and Kame'enui (1987) conducted a study of fourth-grade students with LD and found that the reading comprehension of students who were taught character motive using the direct instruction approach outlined above improved considerably when compared with students with LD using a workbook/discussion group. Using explicit teaching to introduce and support students' generation of theme and character motive assists them in understanding the main idea of what they are read.

Rule Statement

Teacher: Listen. Here is a rule about motive.

The reason a character does something is called motive.

Listen again. The character motive is the reason a character does something in a story.

Your turn. Say the rule about character motive.

The character motive is the reason a character does something in a story.

Repeat until firm.

Individual Test

Call on students to state the rule about character motive.
    1. Demonstration of Examples

Teacher: We will find the character motive of a story together.

First listen to the story, and then we will find the character motive.

Here is the story. Listen.

It was late. Jim was mad. The bus was not on its way. Jim stomped his foot and said, "I didn't really want to go on the bus anyway."

    2. Multiple Procedure

Teacher: Everybody.

 Who is this story about?

Students: *Jim.*

T: Everybody.

 What is Jim doing?

S: *Waiting for a bus.*

T: Everybody.

 How does Jim feel?

S: *Mad.*

T: Everybody.

 Why was he mad?

S: *Because the bus was late.*

T: Everybody.

 How do you know he was mad?

S: *He stomped his foot.*

T: Everybody.

 Why did he say he did not want to ride on the bus?

S: *Because the bus was late.*

T: Everybody.

 Did Jim say what he meant?

S: *No.*

(continued)

FIGURE 5.6. An example of a rule-based instructional strategy. Rabren, Darch, and Eaves (1999). Copyright 1999 by PRO-ED. Reprinted by permission.

T: Everybody.

  What did Jim really want to do?

S: *Ride on the bus.*

T: My turn, listen carefully.

  The character motive is the reason a character does something.

  Jim wanted to ride the bus but he said he didn't because he was mad.

T: Your turn.

S: *The character motive is the reason a character does something.*

S: *Jim wanted to ride the bus, but he said he didn't because he was mad.*

Repeat until firm.

FIGURE 5.6. *(continued)*

CONCLUSION

Teachers can feel confident that the time put into planning and implementing the strategies presented in this chapter will help students understand and remember what they read. As Mastropieri and Scruggs (1997) reported, students with LD can improve their reading comprehension if teachers:

- Teach strategies that have been documented as effective in promoting reading comprehension.
- Design instruction based on effective principles of direct instruction and strategy instruction.
- Provide modeling, support, guided instruction, practice, attributional feedback, and opportunities to practice across text types.
- Monitor students' progress and make adjustments accordingly.

Stories of students who feel actively engaged in reading for meaning remind us of the importance of supporting students in their text comprehension. Students tell us that they want to understand what they read, and they like it when they are given the tools to do so. In a classroom recently, we asked students what they thought of the new reading comprehension strategies their teacher was using. A quiet student with a reading disability slowly raised her hand and responded, "Before, my teacher did all the talking. Now I know ways to figure it [what I read] out on my own, and I can tell *her* what the story is about."

READING COMPREHENSION SAMPLE LESSON PLANS
(to Accompany Chapter 5)

TEXT PREVIEW

Grade Levels

All

Purpose

To introduce a new text, engage students, and focus reading.

Materials

Text
Prepared preview

Lesson

1. Provide a context for the new reading and its relation to what students have already learned. This information activates prior knowledge about the subject and guides students to make explicit connections between what they already know and what they will learn.
2. Provide a quote or bit of interesting information from the reading to motivate readers to find out more about the topic.
3. Ask one to three focus questions to guide readers to attend to the important information during reading.

Following is an example of a teacher preview in a sixth-grade social studies class.

Context

In this unit we have been studying the civil rights movement and looking at ways that people use words and actions, instead of fighting, to get their ideas to be heard. We have talked about Dr. Martin Luther King, Jr. and read several biographies and speeches. Today we are going to learn about another important man who used nonviolent ways to help people. His name is Mahatma Gandhi. Some of you may have heard of him; there are many books and even a few movies about him. Today we will read a story about Gandhi's life and his influence in Africa and in the world.

Engage

Here is a famous quote from Gandhi that is part of your reading today: "In the empire of nonviolence, every true thought counts, every true voice has its face value."

Questions

While you are reading, I want you to think about this quote and the following questions: (1) What are examples of nonviolent ways that Gandhi influenced people? (2) What might have happened if Gandhi had used fighting and violence? (3) What does it mean when he says "every true thought counts, every true voice has its face value"?

Adaptation for Students with Special Needs

1. For students who struggle with auditory processing or remaining focused during reading, provide an outline of the teacher preview and guiding questions.
2. Adjust the number of focus questions for students. Whereas some students may be able to attend to several key questions while reading, others should focus on just one important question that is specific to individual skills, such as remembering factual information, making a personal connection to reading, or drawing conclusions.
3. Students who would benefit from additional practice reading can preread the selection and prepare a "teacher preview." The teacher collaborates with students to prepare the class teacher preview. Students benefit by having an additional opportunity to read. Their preread is focused when they attempt to situate the reading, find an engaging piece of information, and ask their own questions.

WHAT DO YOU KNOW?

Grade Levels

All

Purpose

To increase comprehension and memory of key ideas by asking questions about what you read.

Materials

Reading passage
Index cards
Prepared *What do you know?* materials (dollar amount cards, category headings, timer, score keeping materials)

Lesson

Note: This lesson is used with students who are familiar with writing questions about what they read.

1. Students read a passage and then write questions with a partner in specific teacher-selected question categories that will be used during the *What do you know?* question game. Questions can be arranged by topic area (e.g., dates, travel information, about the explorers), by question type (e.g., Right There, Think and Search, Author and You) or by other categories related to the topic or skills you are addressing in class.
2. Students use index cards to write questions and their answers in the selected categories.

3. The teacher collects and organizes the questions and puts up the game board. The sample game below (which can be drawn on the board) has questions organized by QAR question type.

Right There	Think and Search	Author and You
$10	$20	$30
$10	$20	$30
$10	$20	$30
$10	$20	$30
$10	$20	$30

4. To play the game, students form heterogeneous groups of four or five. A group selects a question type, and the teacher asks the question. The group is given a specified amount of time to confer and agree on the answer. The teacher may call on any of the group members to give the group's answer, so everyone is accountable. If a group does not have the correct answer, another group may attempt the answer. Points are awarded accordingly.
5. Additional hints:
   - Many teachers find it useful to have group work rules to manage students during this activity. For example, if students are noisy or are not working cooperatively, they may have to pay a $10 fine that is deducted from their group's score.
   - Teachers may also elect to add a few of their own questions to be sure that key ideas are reviewed.
   - If one or more of the questions are particularly important or difficult, teachers can label them as bonus questions. When a bonus question is pulled, all groups work on the answer (ensuring that everyone knows the information) and write down an answer. Any group who gets the correct answer receives points for that question.
   - Be creative! This activity is a fun way to (1) encourage students to ask questions as they read and (2) to review and remember information about what has been read.

Adaptation for Students with Special Needs

1. During question asking, students can be required to write questions in specific question types (e.g., three Think and Search questions), allowing students with good question-asking skills to come up with more challenging questions. Likewise, you can vary the number of questions that students are required to ask, provide question stems, or limit the amount of text used to generate questions.
2. Allow students who struggle with comprehension to preview some of the questions and find the answers in the text prior to the whole-class game. Select 5–10 of the questions with important information for this practice activity.
3. Vary the way students find the answers according to individual needs. For example, students can use the text or be required to know the information and answer the questions from memory. Another variation is for all students in the group to find the answer and write it down prior to coming to a group consensus to give everyone the time to search for the answer before the fastest student blurts out a response.

MAIN IDEA SKETCH

Grade Levels

All

Purpose

To use drawing to help students conceptualize and remember the main idea of what they read. This strategy works well with narrative text.

Materials

Short passages
Paper and pencil

Lesson

1. Model the strategy.

- Read a passage aloud from a short story.
- Think aloud about the main idea of the passage by using the following guides:
  - What is the most important *who* or *what*?
  - What is the most important thing about the *who* or *what*?
- Draw a quick sketch of the main idea.
- Write a main idea statement under the sketch.
- If students need additional clarification, repeat with another passage.

2. Provide guided practice.
   - Now read another passage out loud while students follow along in their own text. Have students draw their own main idea sketch, including a main idea caption.
   - Ask students to share drawings and explain their thinking.

3. Apply the strategy individually or in partners.

- As students become more adept at drawing a response, they can work independently or in partners to read a section or chapter, draw the main idea, and then write a main idea caption. The length of the main idea caption will vary depending on the amount of text. For example, the main idea caption for one paragraph of reading should contain about 10 words or less, whereas a chapter in a novel might contain several sentences.
- Debrief with students by sharing drawings and discussing them with the class. Ask students to think about how their drawings influenced their understanding of what they read. Do they think they were able to remember what they read better after they made their drawings? After doing a few main idea sketches, did students find themselves creating more mental images as they read?

Adaptation for Students with Special Needs

1. Students who struggle to come up with the main idea will need extra opportunities to practice the strategy with guided feedback. Be sure students understand and can apply the strategy before they are asked to use it independently during reading.

2. Some students take a long time to draw, limiting the amount of time they have to read. Stress that these are quick sketches (use pen to limit erasures, if necessary) to help students gather ideas and remember what they read. Limit amount of space for drawings or set a time limit for drawings (e.g., 5 minutes to draw and write main idea caption) to guide students to use this skill efficiently.

3. For students who need more explicit instruction, break the task into steps.
   a. Look at the main idea picture (created by the student or provided by the teacher) and think about how it relates to the reading.
   b. What is the most important *who* or *what*? _____
   c. What is the most important thing about the *who* or *what*? _____
   _____
   d. Write your main idea caption. _____

4. If students continue to struggle to identify the main idea after modeling and guided practice, scaffold their strategy use by providing the main idea statement and having them draw a picture of it. Then create the sketch and ask students to write the main idea. Repeat as needed to support students in learning this valuable strategy.

CHAPTER 6

Multicomponent Approaches to Strategy Instruction

1. Before reading this chapter, discuss with your colleagues examples of "multicomponent" strategies that you may have implemented or with which you are familiar. Have you or has someone in your group already tried reciprocal teaching? Collaborative strategic reading? Transactional strategies instruction? What were your impressions?

2. As you read, think about which multicomponent approaches to strategy instruction would make the most sense to try with your students, and why.

3. After reading this chapter, discuss with your study group what you learned about multicomponent approaches to strategy instruction and how this information might help you support your students' reading comprehension.

4. Try out an approach with your students for a minimum of 4 weeks. Be sure to collect student outcome data as part of this process. Share your impressions of the approach with your colleagues.

In our closing chapter we describe three comprehensive instructional approaches designed to help students become strategic readers by applying strategies before, during, and after reading. These approaches are reciprocal teaching, transactional strategies instruction, and collaborative strategic reading. These multicomponent approaches combine aspects of the different methods for promoting reading comprehension we have already described in this book. We present them here because they offer a way to pull everything together and help students apply comprehension strategies while they are learning content from expository text or reading novels, short stories, or other narrative texts.

All three methods rely on peer discussion as a catalyst for improving comprehension. Notably, Fall, Webb, and Chudowsky (2000) recently compared student performance on a high-stakes language arts test when students either were or were not permitted to discuss with peers the story they were being asked to read and interpret. Results showed that a 10-minute discussion of a story in three-person groups had a substantial impact on students' understanding of what they had read.

RECIPROCAL TEACHING

Developed by Palincsar and Brown (1984; Palincsar, 1986; Palincsar, Brown, & Martin, 1987), reciprocal teaching was originally designed to improve comprehension for middle school students who could decode but had difficulty comprehending text. Students learn to use the four strategies of prediction, summarization, question generation, and clarification and to apply these while discussing text with the teacher and their peers. The teacher first models how to implement the strategies. Next, through prompts, questions, and reminders, the teacher supports students' efforts to use the strategies while reading and discussing text. As students become more proficient, the teacher gradually reduces this assistance. The premise is that teaching students to use the four strategies collaboratively in a dialogue will help them bring meaning to the text as well as promote their internalization of the use of the strategies—thus ultimately improving their reading comprehension.

Theoretical Foundation

Brown and Palincsar (1989) described three related theories that explain effectiveness of reciprocal teaching: the zone of proximal development, scaffolding, and proleptic teaching. In the zone of proximal development (Vygotsky, 1978), the focus is not on what students can do independently but on how students' emerging skills and knowledge can be enhanced with guidance provided through interactions with others. The manner in which support is provided within a student's zone of proximal development is based on the theories of scaffolding (Wood, Bruner, & Ross, 1976) and proleptic teaching (Rogoff & Gardner, 1984). Palincsar and Brown (1989, p. 411) described scaffolding as a means of providing "adjustable and temporary supports" through which the expert guides the learner to solve a problem that he or she would not be able to complete independently, much as a construction scaffold provides temporary support to builders. In order to successfully assist the learner, the expert must be aware of where the child's abilities lie on a continuum from novice to expert and be able to adjust instruction accordingly. Proleptic teaching means setting high expectations for all students, regardless of their current level of functioning. In this approach the teacher acts as the expert while the child takes on an apprentice role.

Reciprocal teaching is also firmly grounded in cognitive views of learning and development (Brown & Palincsar, 1989). Students are presented with multiple models of cognitive processing, through explanations and think-alouds, from the teacher and their peers. In addition, each of the four reciprocal teaching strategies can be explained in terms of cognitive psychology: prediction (Stauffer, 1969), question generation (Manzo, 1968), clarification (Markman, 1985), and summarization (Brown & Day, 1983). Similarly, the idea of using metacognition to monitor one's use of strategies and understanding of what is being read comes from cognitive psychology (Flavell, 1979).

Research Support

In their first pioneering study, Palincsar and Brown (1984) taught comprehension strategies to seventh graders who were adequate decoders but poor comprehenders. Students participated in approximately 20 sessions. Each session included strategy instruction as well as an assessment of how many questions they could answer accurately after reading a short passage. Students in a control condition took the same pretests and posttests as did the strategy-instructed students but received no strategy instruction or daily assessments. Students who participated in the reciprocal teaching intervention outperformed comparison students on all measures of text comprehension and memory.

Since Palincsar and Brown's (1984) initial study, other researchers have also investigated reciprocal teaching. In comparison with traditional methods, reciprocal teaching has been found to be more effective, using both narrative and expository texts, with a wide range of students: middle school English language learners with LD, including low decoders (Klingner & Vaughn, 1996), high school students in remedial classes (Alfassi, 1998), and average and above-average readers at various grade levels (Rosenshine & Meister, 1994), including fourth graders (Lysynchuk, Pressley, & Vye, 1990) and fifth graders (King & Parent Johnson, 1999). Rosenshine and Meister (1994) reviewed 16 studies on reciprocal teaching and found that it consistently yielded statistically significant findings on different measures of reading comprehension. An important finding was that reciprocal teaching was more successful when it included direct teaching of the four comprehension strategies.

In other studies, researchers have combined reciprocal teaching with other approaches or compared it with different methods. For example, Marston, Deno, Kim, Diment, and Rogers (1995) compared six research-based teaching strategies, including reciprocal teaching, and found that student achievement was highest with the following three approaches: computer-assisted instruction, reciprocal teaching, and one of two direct instruction conditions. Johnson-Glenberg (2000) trained third- through fifth-grade adequate decoders who were poor comprehenders for 10 weeks in either reciprocal teaching or a visualization program. The reciprocal teaching group excelled on measures that depended on explicit, factual material, whereas the visualization group did best on visually mediated measures.

Brand-Gruwal, Aarnoutse, and Van Den Bos (1997) provided reciprocal teaching plus direct instruction in comprehension strategies to 9- to 11-year-olds who were poor in decoding, reading comprehension, and listening comprehension. The researchers found positive effects for strategic variables but not for general reading comprehension.

Klingner and Vaughn (1996) studied 26 seventh- and eighth-grade students with LD who were English language learners. Students learned a modified version of reciprocal teaching that included an emphasis on accessing background knowledge. Students read English text but were encouraged to use both Spanish (their native language) and English in their discussions. An important finding was that a continuum of students, rather than just those students who were adequate decoders but poor comprehenders, benefited from reciprocal teaching. In other words, students who had comprehension levels higher than their decoding skills also made gains in reading comprehension. In addition, Klingner and Vaughn reported that students continued making gains even when they worked in small groups or in tutoring dyads without the immediate presence of the researcher as teacher.

How to Implement Reciprocal Teaching

Reciprocal teaching includes three essential components: dialogue, comprehension strategies, and scaffolding. The dialogue begins after students read a paragraph from the assigned text. The teacher or a student in the role of "dialogue leader" then begins a discussion structured around the four reading strategies. The dialogue leader is responsible for starting the discussion by asking questions and helping the group clarify any words or concepts that are unclear. Answering questions, elaborating or commenting on others' answers, and asking new questions are the responsibility of everyone in the group. The dialogue leader then provides a summary of the paragraph and invites the group to elaborate or comment on the summary. The dialogue leader also gives or asks for predictions about the upcoming paragraph. Through this process the group is able to move beyond merely restating the information in the text to develop a collective meaning for the passage. After the dialogue is finished, the process begins again with a new section of text and a new leader.

At the heart of the dialogue are the four strategies: questioning, clarifying, summarizing, and predicting. Palincsar and Brown (1984) selected these strategies because they are the tactics good readers use to make sense of text. Figure 6.1 provides a description, rationale, and method for each of the four strategies.

The scaffolding of instruction is integral to reciprocal teaching. The teacher guides students in using the strategies and gradually turns over this responsibility of strategy application to the students themselves. First the teacher explains the purpose for learning comprehension strategies, telling students that the primary goal is for them to become better readers (i.e., more "strategic" and better comprehenders). Following this purpose-setting statement, the teacher models the entire process of reading a passage and applying the strategies by using think-

Predicting

1. *Description*: Predicting involves finding clues in the structure and content of a passage that might suggest what will happen next.
2. *Rationale*: Predicting activates prior knowledge and motivates students to continue reading the passage to determine if their predictions were correct.
3. *Method*: To learn this strategy, students are instructed to use the title to make initial predictions about the story and then to use clues in the story to make additional predictions before reading each new paragraph or section of text. Students share predictions with one another.

Clarifying

1. *Description*: Clarifying involves discerning when there is a breakdown in comprehension and taking steps to restore meaning.
2. *Rationale*: Clarifying assures that the passage will make sense to the reader.
3. *Method*: To learn this strategy, students are instructed to be alert to occasions when they are not understanding the meaning of text, and when this occurs to process the text again. For instance, if a word did not make sense to the student, he or she would be instructed to try to define the word by reading the sentences that precede and follow it. Students are also taught to attend to words such as *or*, which may signal the meaning of an unfamiliar word, and to be certain they know to what referents such as *them*, *it*, and *they* refer (anaphora). If, after rereading the passage, something is still not clear, students are instructed to request assistance.

Summarizing

1. *Description*: A summary is a one- or two-sentence statement that tells the most important ideas contained in a paragraph or section of text. The summary should contain only the most important ideas and should not include unimportant details. A summary should be in the student's own words.
2. *Rationale*: Summarizing can improve understanding and memory of what is read.
3. *Method*: Students are instructed to locate the topic sentence of a paragraph. If there is no topic sentence, they are taught to make up their own topic sentence by combining the sentences they have underlined as containing the most relevant ideas. Students are then instructed to locate the most important details that support the topic sentence and to delete what is unimportant or redundant. Finally, they are instructed to restate the main idea and supporting details in their own words.

Question Generating

1. *Description*: Questions are constructed about important information, rather than about unimportant details, in the text.
2. *Rationale*: Question generation allows readers to self-test their understanding of the text and helps them to identify what is important in the story.
3. *Method*: To learn this strategy, students are instructed to select important information from the paragraph and use the words *who, how, when, where*, and *why* to make up questions. Students are taught to ask questions about the main idea of the passage, questions about important details, and questions for which the passage does not provide the answer.

FIGURE 6.1. Reciprocal teaching strategies.

alouds so that students can see "the big picture." The teacher may next choose to provide direct instruction in each of the strategies before proceeding. The teacher and students then use the strategies while reading and discussing text in small groups. The teacher offers a great deal of support as students try to implement the strategies. The teacher must be skillful at assessing the students' zone of proximal development and adjusting support accordingly, using scaffolding techniques such as prompts, elaborations, modifications, praise, and feedback. The teacher is the first dialogue leader, but as students develop proficiency in applying the strategies, they then take turns leading discussions. This approach sets high expectations for all the students—a basic feature of proleptic teaching. By about the eighth day of reciprocal teaching, in their alternating roles as students and dialogue leaders, students typically can implement the strategies with minimal assistance from the teacher. See Figure 6.2 for a step-by-step guide for how to implement reciprocal teaching. Note that this model includes direct instruction in the strategies.

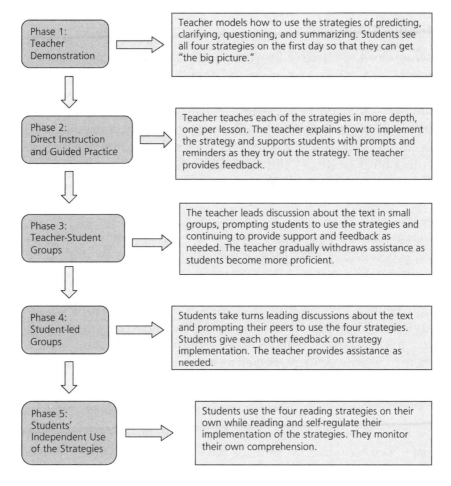

FIGURE 6.2. How to implement reciprocal teaching. Data from Palincsar and Brown (1984) and Quezada, Williams, and Flores (2006).

TRANSACTIONAL STRATEGIES INSTRUCTION

Pressley and colleagues (Pressley, El-Dinary, et al., 1992; Pressley, Schuder, et al., 1992; Pressley, Brown, El-Dinary, & Afflerbach, 1995) developed a comprehensive, high-intensity, long-term approach to strategy implementation called *transactional strategies instruction*. As with reciprocal teaching, in the transactional approach to strategy instruction the teacher provides support and guidance to students as they apply strategies while interacting with text and learning content. Through teacher explanation, modeling, and supported practice, students learn to use repertoires of comprehension strategies. A central goal of instruction is the self-regulated use of the strategies. The term *transactional* is used to emphasize that (1) meaning is determined through the interaction of prior knowledge and information conveyed through print; (2) one person's reaction is influenced by what other group members do, think, and say; and (3) the meaning that emerges is the product of the group's interactions (Pressley et al., 1995).

Theoretical Foundation

The underpinnings of strategy instruction can be found in cognitive psychology (Pressley & Hilden, 2006). Cognitive psychology focuses on what happens in the brain during cognitive activity. The execution of strategies can be cognitively demanding. Therefore, using strategies can use up a lot of short-term capacity that then is not available for other tasks. The more proficient a person is in applying strategies, the less cognitive capacity is consumed, leaving more capacity for implementing other strategies and for coordination with other cognitive activities. Capable readers use comprehension strategies efficiently—indeed, almost effortlessly. The implications for instruction from cognitive psychology are that:

- Students learn the strategies used by capable thinkers to accomplish tasks.
- Instruction begins with explanations and modeling of strategies, followed by supported practice.
- Strategy practice typically continues for a long time, until the strategy can be implemented with little effort, across a variety of situations, and is self-regulated.
- Strategy instruction includes metacognitive information about when and where to use the strategy, as well as how to monitor its effectiveness of strategies.

Transactional strategies instruction goes beyond cognitive psychology, though, by acknowledging the importance of others in the learning process and putting even greater emphasis on the role of background knowledge. Pressley (1998) describes three different theories that contributed to the notion of *transactional* in this approach. The first is Rosenblatt's (1978) reader response theory. Rosenblatt used the term *transactional* to emphasize that meaning does not reside in the text alone or in the reader's head alone, but rather is constructed by readers as they contemplate text content in light of their previous knowledge and experiences. In developmental psychology (Bell, 1968), the term *transactional* refers to the importance of interactions with others during the learning process, in the sense that a child's actions in part determine the behaviors of the adults and others around him or her. Finally, organizational psychology (Hutchins, 1991) suggests that the meaning that emerges as teachers and students use strategies together to read and comprehend a text is collaboratively produced by everyone in the group.

Research Support

Pressley and colleague's initial studies were conducted at Benchmark School, a facility that is dedicated to educating students with reading disabilities. In one early study they interviewed teachers to find out their beliefs about strategy instruction (Pressley et al., 1991). In another study, Gaskins, Anderson, Pressley, Cunicelli, and Satlow (1993) watched the strategy instruction lessons of six teachers at Benchmark and analyzed classroom discourse. They noted how different the dialogue was in the Benchmark classrooms in comparison with traditional classrooms, in which the most common form of discourse is for the teacher to ask a question, a student to respond, and the teacher to provide an evaluative comment (i.e., an initiation, response, evaluation, or IRE, sequence; see Cazden, 1988). Gaskins et al. developed a list of the most common instructional events they observed:

- Teachers explained how to carry out the strategies.
- Teachers modeled the strategies.
- Teachers identified the target strategy of a given lesson early for students.
- Teachers presented information about why the target strategy was important.
- Teachers provided information about when and where strategies would apply.
- Students practiced strategies with as-needed teacher guidance over a long period.

El Dinary, Pressley, and Schuder (1992) continued their investigations of effective comprehension instruction in Maryland county schools and found that when transactional strategies were used, teacher and student behaviors were quite similar to those observed at Benchmark School. Pressley, Schuder, et al. (1992) identified the following common features of effective strategy instruction:

1. Strategy instruction is long term and integrated with ongoing instruction. Comprehension strategies are taught during language arts and applied in math, science, social studies, and other content areas.
2. Teachers assure that students understand the connection between active,

strategic thinking and academic success. Students learn when and where use of strategies "pays off."

3. Effective strategy instruction emphasizes the flexible application of a repertoire of strategies rather than the use of single strategies.

4. Strategies are introduced one at a time and applied through reading text. Teachers explain strategies and model their use. They scaffold students' efforts to apply strategies by providing hints and additional explanations as needed.

5. Discussions of how students use strategies to process text occur every day. Much of strategy instruction occurs in small groups, with students thinking aloud as they read and apply strategies. Ideal discussions are dynamic, with students reacting, interpreting, and offering alternative points of view.

6. Students learn that readers respond to text differently, depending on their background experiences and interpretations of the text. How an individual reacts to text is also influenced by what other participants in a group do and say about the text. The co-constructed meaning that emerges from a group is the product of all the persons in that group.

Three research studies validated the effectiveness of transactional strategies instruction. Brown, Pressley, Van Meter, and Schuder (1996) conducted a year long-quasi-experimental investigation of the effects of transactional strategies instruction in second-grade classrooms with low-achieving readers. End-of-the-year testing showed that students in the transactional strategies instruction classrooms improved significantly more than other students on a standardized reading comprehension test as well as on other measures. Also, they learned more content. Over the course of one semester in fifth- and sixth-grade classrooms, Collins (1991) reported that students who participated in reading comprehension strategy lessons improved significantly. Similarly, Anderson (1992) conducted a 3-month investigation of transactional strategies instruction with students with reading disabilities in grades 6–11 and found that students who learned comprehension strategies made greater gains than those who did not. In addition, students who learned strategies were more willing to read challenging material, collaborate with classmates during reading, and respond to text.

How to Implement Transactional Strategies Instruction

Similar to reciprocal teaching and collaborative strategic reading, transactional strategies instruction consists of three phases (Casteel, Isom, & Jordan, 2000):

1. *Explanation and modeling:* It is helpful for the teacher to make posters or displays for each of the strategies and post them on the wall where students can easily see them. Then the teacher selects a strategy to teach. The teacher defines and explains the selected strategy to students and models its usage. Then he or she emphasizes why the strategy is helpful and explains when it might be most appropriate to use it.

2. *Practice and coaching:* Next the teacher provides students with opportunities for guided practice and feedback. The teacher coaches as necessary, possibly asking questions such as What do you do next? How is the strategy helpful? During this phase the teacher provides students with practice in implementing the strategies as well as in selecting which strategy to use at different times.

3. *Transfer of responsibility:* Once students have become proficient strategy users, then they can use various strategies while reading, monitoring their understanding, and discussing the meaning of text in small reading groups. They assume responsibility for selecting and implementing strategies. The teacher continues to coach students as they use various strategies as they work in their groups.

Unlike the approaches of reciprocal teaching and collaborative strategic reading, in which students are taught only a set number of strategies (usually about four), students learn numerous strategies in transactional strategies instruction and are taught to apply them flexibly. In Table 6.1 we describe six of these strategies and how to teach them during the "practice and coaching" phase of instruction (Casteel et al., 2000; Pressley, 1998).

Once students have developed some proficiency in applying the strategies through whole-class instruction, much of the strategy implementation takes place in small groups in which students engage in meaningful conversations about the text they are reading. Students discuss their predictions, interpretive images, questions, summaries, and reflections about how to deal with difficult aspects of the text.

The Students Achieving Independent Learning (SAIL) program represents an effective application of transactional strategies instruction (Bergman, 1992; Pressley, Schuder, SAIL faculty and administration, Bergman, & El-Dinary, 1992). The SAIL program promotes extensive reading of children's literature and encourages students to set their own purposes and goals for reading. A prominently displayed chart serves to remind students of the questions they can ask themselves as they read (see Figure 6.3).

COLLABORATIVE STRATEGIC READING

With collaborative strategic reading (CSR), students learn to use comprehension strategies that support their understanding of expository text (Klingner, Vaughn, Dimino, Schumm, & Bryant, 2001; Klingner & Vaughn, 1999). The development of CSR was influenced significantly by the approaches of reciprocal teaching and transactional strategies instruction. Initially, the teacher presents the strategies to the whole class using modeling, role playing, and teacher think-alouds. After students have developed proficiency in using the strategies, the teacher then assigns the students to heterogeneous cooperative learning groups (Johnson & Johnson, 1989; Kagan, 1991). Each student performs a defined role while collaboratively implementing the strategies. Hence, with CSR, all students are actively involved, and everyone has the opportunity to contribute as group members learn from and understand the text. See Table 6.2 for a comparison of reciprocal teaching and CSR.

TABLE 6.1. Six Strategies of Transactional Stratsegies Instruction and How to Teach Them during the "Practice and Coaching" Phase of Instruction

Name of strategy	What students do	How to teach the strategy
Predicting	Students predict what they think a selection will be about or what they will learn. During reading, they can modify their predictions if they choose. After reading, they verify if their predications were correct.	• Ask students what they already know about the topic. • Teach students to read the title, skim the text, and look at headings before making their predictions. • Ask students what information they used to come up with their predictions. • Have students modify their predictions as they learn new information while reading. • Teach students to check the accuracy of their predictions after reading. • Ask students to think about how helpful it is to predict.
Questioning and answering	Students answer questions about the passage. The teacher may ask questions about the text at key points during and after reading. Or students may generate questions, either before reading, about what they would like to learn, or after reading, about key points. Students identify the question–answer relationships (Raphael, 1986) and answer the questions.	• Teach students to identify different types of questions (see Chapter 5) and the strategy for finding the answer to each. • "Right There"—Find the answer in one place in the book. • "Think and Search"—Find the answer in more than one place in the book. • "Author and Me"—Find the answer in the book and in your head. • "On My Own"—Answer the question using what you already know about the topic. • Teach students how to generate questions using these same question types.
Visualizing	Students construct mental images that represent text content. Extension: Students construct graphic representations of their mental images.	• Teach students to visualize the content in a passage or imagine what is happening. • For stories, have students visualize what is happening at the beginning, middle, and end of the story. • For informational text, have students think about key words and visualize the content they are learning. • Ask students to explain their images. • Have students compare the picture in their minds with what they are reading. • Extension: Have students draw diagrams or pictures to represent their visualizations.
Seeking clarifications	During reading, students monitor their understanding. When the text does not make sense, the student selects a strategy to help clarify the confusing text.	• Teach students to check their understanding while reading. At first, frequently ask students, "Does this make sense?" Encourage students to do the same. • Teach students to select a strategy to use to fix comprehension when breakdowns occur. These can include: • Ignore and read on. • Guess, using clues from the context. • Reread for clarification. • Look back in the text for clues that can help. • Ask students to explain why they selected the strategy they did, and if it helped.
Responding to text based on prior knowledge	Students make connections between the text and their background knowledge and personal experiences.	• Ask students to tell how the information from the passage relates to their own lives. • Ask students how the information might be important to them and how it might help them.

(continued)

TABLE 6.1. *(continued)*

Name of strategy	What students do	How to teach the sxstrategy
		• Encourage students to discuss their ideas with one another. Ask how considering different points of view can broaden their knowledge.

Summarizing	After reading, students summarize the passage. For informational text, they restate the most important ideas. For narrative text, they retell the story.
	
	Extension: For expository text, students identify the text structure (e.g., compare and contrast, sequence) and use this structure as a way to organize summaries.
		• Teach students to differentiate between expository and narrative texts.
		  • When retelling a story, have students describe the setting, characters, problem, events (in order), and the solution.
		  • For expository text, have students restate the main ideas in the passage.
		
		Extension: Teach students about different text structures (see Chapter 4) and how to use these as organizational structures for expository text summaries.

Questions I Can Ask as I Read
- To get the main idea
- What is the story about?
- What is the problem?
- What is the solution?
- What makes me think so?

To predict–verify–decide
- What's going to happen next?
- Is my prediction still good?
- Do I need to change my prediction?
- What makes me think so?

To visualize–verify–decide
- What does this (person, place, thing) look like?
- Is the picture in my mind still good?
- Do I need to change my picture?
- What makes me think so?

To summarize
- What has happened so far?
- What makes me think so?

To think aloud
- What am I thinking?
- Why?

To solve problems or help when I don't understand
- Shall I guess?
- Ignore and read on?
- Reread and look back?
- Why?

FIGURE 6.3. Question chart for transactional strategies instruction. Adapted from Bergman (1992). Copyright 1992 by The International Reading Association. Adapted by permission.

TABLE 6.2. How CSR and Reciprocal Teaching Differ

Reciprocal teaching	Collaborative strategic reading
Designed for use with narrative as well as expository text.	Designed primarily for use with expository text.
No *brainstorming before reading.*	Students *brainstorm to activate prior knowledge as part of preview (before reading).*
Students *predict what they think will happen next before reading each paragraph or segment of text.*	Students only *predict as part of the preview strategy (before reading), making informed hunches about what they think they will learn.*
Students *clarify words or chunks of text they don't understand by rereading the sentences before and after the sentence they don't understand, and/or asking a peer for assistance.*	Students use "fix-up strategies" to clarify *"clunks" (words they don't understand):* • Reread the sentence. • Reread the sentences before and after. • Break apart the work and look for smaller words you know. • Look for a prefix or suffix you know.
Students *summarize the paragraph or segment of text they have just read.*	Students *get the gist of the paragraph or segment of text they have just read, identifying "the most important who or what"* and the most important thing about the *who* or *what.* They say the gist in 10 words or less.
Students *generate questions after each paragraph or segment of text they have just read.*	Students only *generate questions as part of a wrap-up after they have read the entire day's selection. Students answer each other's questions.*
There is no *review after reading.*	Students *review what they have learned after reading the day's selection.*
There are eight to 12 students, plus the teacher, in the group.	An entire class is divided into *cooperative groups of two to five; the teacher circulates rather than staying with one group.*
There are no learning logs.	Students record their previews, clunks, questions, and what they've learned in individual *CSR learning logs.*
The "leader" (a student) facilitates the discussion about a paragraph or section of text; this role rotates after each paragraph.	Every student in the group has a meaningful role; one of these roles is to be the "leader." Roles are assigned for an entire lesson (only rotating biweekly in some classes).
There are no cue cards.	Students use *cue cards to help them implement their roles and the comprehension strategies.*

The goals of CSR are to improve reading comprehension and increase conceptual learning in ways that maximize students' participation. Originally developed to help English language learners and students with learning disabilities become more confident, competent readers in heterogeneous "mainstream" classrooms, CSR has also proven to be a valuable approach for students at varying achievement levels. CSR provides students with a more independent way to interact with grade-level textbooks and learn important content than, for example, a whole-class, teacher-led approach that involves reading the text and answering the questions at the end of the chapter.

We introduce the four strategies students learn as part of CSR here and describe them in more detail later:

1. *Preview*: Prior to reading a passage, students recall what they already know about the topic and predict what the passage might be about.
2. *Click and clunk*: Students monitor comprehension during reading by identifying difficult words and concepts in the passage and using fix-up strategies when the text does not make sense.
3. *Get the gist*: During reading, students restate the most important idea in a paragraph or section.
4. *Wrap-up*: After reading, students summarize what has been learned and generate questions "that a teacher might ask on a test."

Theoretical Foundation

Like reciprocal teaching (Palincsar & Brown 1984), CSR is grounded in sociocultural theory and the principles of scaffolding, zone of proximal development (Vygotsky, 1978), and cognitive psychology (Flavell, 1992). The idea is that cognitive development occurs when concepts first learned through social interaction become internalized and made one's own. Through the collaborative approach emphasized with CSR, learning is scaffolded by both teacher and students. The teacher provides instruction in strategies, assigns group roles, and provides a guide for reading and discussion. Students then scaffold each others' learning by providing immediate feedback at a level and in a manner that is just right for the others in the group.

CSR capitalized on this theoretical heritage and extended it to reflect knowledge about teaching English language learners and students with reading disabilities. One way CSR extended this approach was by helping students tap into their prior knowledge (Fitzgerald, 1995) and make connections with their own lives (Perez, 1998). Also, CSR takes into account that students with learning disabilities and English language learners benefit from explicit instruction. Therefore, the teacher carefully teaches the strategies using clear explanations and lots of modeling. He or she provides students with multiple opportunities to practice the strategies in supported situations before asking them to apply the strategies on their own in cooperative learning groups.

Research Support

Over a 10-year period, CSR has yielded positive outcomes for students with learning disabilities and those at risk for reading difficulties, as well as average and high-achieving students (Bryant, Vaughn, Linan-Thompson, Ugel, & Hamff, 2000; Klingner, Vaughn, Argüelles, Hughes, & Ahwee, 2004; Klingner, Vaughn, & Schumm, 1998; Vaughn, Chard, et al., 2000) and English language learners (Klingner & Vaughn, 1996, 2000). In the first study of CSR, Klingner et al. (1998) provided instruction in diverse, inclusive fourth-grade classrooms, teaching students how to use CSR while reading social studies text. Comparison students received typical teacher-directed instruction in the same content. CSR students made statistically significant greater gains than students in a control condition on the Gates–MacGinitie Reading Tests and demonstrated equal proficiency in their knowledge of the social studies content.

Klingner and Vaughn (2000) then implemented CSR with fifth-grade students, many of whom were English language learners, while they read and learned from science textbooks in their small groups. Results indicated that students demonstrated high levels of academic engagement and assisted each other with word meanings, main idea, and understanding the text. In other studies, Bryant et al. (2000) implemented CSR in an inclusive middle school program and achieved gains for students with and without disabilities; Vaughn, Chard, et al. (2000) examined the effects of CSR on fluency and comprehension as part of a third-grade intervention, with positive results.

Most recently, Klingner et al. (2004) compared five CSR and five "control" teachers from five schools, along with their students. Students in CSR classrooms improved significantly in reading comprehension when compared with control students. Teachers varied in their implementation of CSR, and, with the exception of one teacher, students' comprehension gains were associated with the quality and quantity of CSR usage.

The most recent adaptation of CSR was a study conducted with middle school students with significant reading difficulties. A computer-adapted approach to using CSR was implemented, in which students worked in pairs to read text on the computer and to respond to the critical CSR strategies (Kim et al., 2006).

Additionally, CSR includes critical elements identified in special education as enhancing the performance of students with disabilities, such as (1) making instruction visible and explicit, (2) implementing procedural strategies to facilitate learning, (3) using interactive groups and/or partners, and (4) providing opportunities for interactive dialogue between students and between teacher and students (Fuchs, Fuchs, Mathes, & Lipsey, 2000; Gersten, Fuchs, Williams, & Baker, 2001; Swanson, Hoskyn, & Lee, 1999; Vaughn, Gersten, & Chard, 2000).

How to Implement Collaborative Strategic Reading

At the outset, the teacher provides explicit instruction to students to teach the CSR reading comprehension strategies. As with reciprocal teaching, the teacher first conveys the value in learning different comprehension strategies, emphasizing that these strategies are what good readers use to help them understand what they read, and that by learning the strategies, everyone can become a better reader. The teacher also emphasizes that reading is thinking. The teacher then uses a think-aloud procedure to model how to use the different strategies while reading a short passage. Again, as with reciprocal teaching, students are exposed to all of the strategies on the first day, so that they can get a sense of CSR-style strategic reading looks like. The teacher then provides additional instruction in each strategy, teaching students why, when, and how to apply each one. The CSR reading strategies include the following (Klingner et al., 2001):

1. *Preview:* The purposes of previewing are to (a) help students identify what the text is about, (b) tap into their prior knowledge about the topic, and (c) generate interest in the topic. The teacher helps the students with previewing by reminding them to use all of the visual clues in the text, such as pictures, charts, or graphs, and to look at the headings and subheadings used throughout the passage. He or she might help them connect the topic to their own experiences and also preteach key vocabulary that is important to understanding the text but that does not lend itself to the click-and-clunk fix-up strategies.

2. *Click and clunk:* Students use the process of click and clunk to monitor their comprehension of the text. When students understand the information, it "clicks"; when it does not make sense, it "clunks." Students work together to identify clunks in the text and use fix-up strategies to help them "declunk" the word or concept. The clunk expert facilitates this process, using clunk cards. A different strategy for figuring out a clunk word, concept, or idea is printed on each card:

   a. Reread the sentence without the word. Think about what would make sense.
   b. Reread the sentence with the clunk and the sentences before or after the clunk, looking for clues.
   c. Look for a prefix or suffix in the word.
   d. Break the word apart and look for smaller words you know.

Students record their clunks in their learning logs to share with their teacher and peers.

3. *Get the gist:* Getting the gist means that students are able to state the main idea of a paragraph or cluster of paragraphs in their own words, as succinctly as possible. In this way students learn how to synthesize information, taking a larger chunk of text and distilling it into a key concept or idea. Students are taught to identify the most important *who* or *what* in the paragraph, and then to identify the most important information they read about the *who* or *what*, leaving out details. Many teachers require that students state the main point of the paragraphs in 10 words or less.

4. *Wrap-up:* Students learn to "wrap-up" by formulating questions and answers about what they have learned and by reviewing key ideas. The goals are to improve students' knowledge, understanding, and memory of what they have read. Students generate questions about important information in the passage. They learn to use question starters to begin their questions: *who, what, when, where, why,* and *how* ("the five Ws and an H"). As with reciprocal teaching, students pretend they are teachers and think of questions they would ask on a test to find out if their students really understood what they had read. Other students should try to answer the questions. Students are taught to ask some questions about information that is stated explicitly in the passage and other questions that require an answer not right in the passage but "in your head" (Raphael, 1986). In other words, students are encouraged to ask questions that involve higher-level thinking skills as

well as literal recall. To review, students write down the most important ideas they learned from the day's reading assignment in their CSR learning logs. They then take turns sharing what they learned with the class. Many students can share their "best idea" in a short period of time, providing the teacher with valuable information about their level of understanding.

Once students are proficient in using the comprehension strategies with the support of the teacher, they are ready to learn how to implement the strategies while working in heterogeneous cooperative learning groups. According to Johnson and Johnson (1989), cooperative learning should encourage and include:

- Positive interdependence
- Considerable face-to-face interaction among students
- Individual accountability
- Positive social skills
- Self as well as group evaluation or reflection

In cooperative groups, students do not simply work together on the same assignment; each person must have a key role to play and everyone is responsible for the success of the group. Students are told that they have two responsibilities: to make sure they learn the material and to help everyone else in their group learn it, too.

Students who have not previously worked in cooperative learning groups may need preparation in order to work productively and effectively in this context. It may be helpful for them to practice skills that are vital for the successful functioning of a group, such as attentive listening, asking for feedback, asking others for their opinion, taking turns, asking clarifying questions, and conflict resolution measures (Klingner et al., 2001; see also Kagan, 1991).

With CSR, students discuss what they have read, assist one another in the comprehension of the text, and provide academic and affective support for their classmates. With CSR everyone has a chance to try out all of the roles. These roles may include (Klingner et al., 2001):

- *Leader*: Leads the group in the implementation of CSR by saying what to read next and what strategy to apply next; asks the teacher for assistance if necessary.
- *Clunk expert*: Uses clunk cards to remind the group of the steps to follow when trying to figure out a difficult word or concept.
- *Gist expert*: Guides the group toward the development of a gist and determines that the gist contains the most important idea(s) but no unnecessary details.
- *Announcer*: Calls on different group members to read or share an idea and makes sure that everyone participates and only one person talks at a time.
- *Encourager*: Watches the group and gives feedback; looks for behaviors to praise; encourages all group members to participate in the discussion and

assist one another; evaluates how well the group has worked together and gives suggestions for improvement.

- *Timekeeper*: Lets group members know how much time they have to write in their learning logs or complete a section of the text they are reading; keeps track of time and reminds the group to stay focused (if necessary).

Many teachers use smaller groups and combine roles and responsibilities, providing explicit instruction in each of the roles. One way to do this is by preteaching the roles to selected students, who can then model them for their classmates. Also, CSR includes cue cards for every role, with prompts that remind students of what is required. Students use the cue cards when first working together in their small groups, but as they become more confident in how to fulfill their roles, they can be encouraged to set aside the cue cards so that more natural discussions can take place. The cue cards serve an important function in that they help students with LD to be successful in any of the CSR roles, including leader.

CSR learning logs are an important component of the model. They enable students to keep track of learning "as it happens" and provide a springboard for follow-up activities. Logs furnish an additional way for all students to participate actively in their groups and provide valuable "wait time" for students with LD and English language learners to form their thoughts. Logs can be used for recording ideas while applying every strategy or only some of the strategies (e.g., for writing down clunks and key ideas). Logs might be kept in spiral-bound notebooks or journals made by folding paper in half and stapling on a construction paper cover. A different learning log can be created for each social studies or science unit; these logs provide written documentation of learning and can serve as excellent study guides. Some special education teachers have even included CSR learning logs in students' IEPs (Chang, & Shimizu, 1997). See Figure 6.4 for an example of a learning log.

Once the teacher has taught the strategies and procedures to students and they have begun working in their cooperative learning groups, the teacher's role is to circulate among the groups and provide ongoing assistance. Teachers can help by actively listening to students' discussion and, if necessary, clarify difficult words, model strategy usage, encourage students to participate, and provide positive reinforcement. Teachers should expect that students will need some assistance learning to work in cooperative groups, implementing the strategies, and mastering the content in textbooks. The focus of students' work should be on learning the material and helping their classmates learn it as well, not merely going through the steps of a given strategy.

CONCLUSION

In conclusion, all three approaches described in this chapter share commonalities, including roots in cognitive psychology and an emphasis on the importance of dia-

Today's Topic _____ Date _____ Name _____

Before Reading:

PREVIEW

What I Already Know about the Topic	After Reading: *WRAP UP*	
	Questions about the Important Ideas in the Passage	
What I Predict I Will Learn	What I Learned	

During Reading

CLUNKS

GISTS

FIGURE 6.4. CSR learning log.

From Janette K. Klingner, Sharon Vaughn, and Alison Boardman. Copyright 2007 by The Guilford Press. Permission to photocopy this figure is granted to purchasers of this book for personal use only (see copyright page for details).

logue with others in promoting learning. With each approach students learn to apply different strategies before, during, and after reading. They learn through modeling, explicit instruction, and guided practice. Each approach has been found to be effective for improving the reading comprehension of students with learning disabilities as well as other students.

In addition, each has been found to be challenging for teachers to learn and apply in their classrooms. We offer this cautionary note in the hopes that teachers will discuss implementation challenges with their colleagues and support one another in trying out new instructional practices. We know that although some teachers seem to catch on quickly and become quite sophisticated strategy instructors, others have trouble getting past surface-level implementation. For example, research suggests that some teachers implement reciprocal teaching ineffectively. "Lethal mutations" can occur, resulting in a less successful technique (Brown & Campione, 1996; Seymour & Osana, 2003). It appears that the goals of reciprocal teaching (i.e., to improve students' self-monitoring and comprehension of the text) and its basic underlying principles are not always fully understood. Similarly, Klingner and colleagues (2004) described the wide variability in CSR implementation among the teachers in their study. They wondered if the ability to teach comprehension strategies well is a higher-level skill, on a hierarchy, and that classroom teachers must first feel comfortable with other aspects of their instruction, such as classroom management, before they can focus on strategy instruction. This idea is reminiscent of cognitive load theory (Valcke, 2002); any individual can focus only on so much at one time.

Pressley and colleagues have written extensively about the challenges of implementing comprehensive strategy instruction programs in real classrooms (Pressley, Hogan, Wharton-McDonald, & Mistretta, 1996; Pressley & El-Dinary, 1997), and Pressley and Hilden (2006) speculate about why it is so hard for some teachers to become masterful strategy instructors. They hypothesized that it is so difficult to teach comprehension strategies well because each strategy is conceptually complex, requiring multiple operations to execute; when put together in a package, multiple strategies become even more complicated. Another hypothesis is that if teachers do not use comprehension strategies themselves or are not aware of their own strategic thinking, they cannot understand them well enough to teach them and may not recognize how much comprehension strategies can improve reading (Keene & Zimmermann, 1997). Instructional activities such as thinking aloud become especially difficult. Pressley and Hilden added that anecdotal evidence suggests that teachers who learn to teach comprehension strategies themselves become more active, strategic readers and better comprehenders (e.g., Pressley, El-Dinary, et al., 1992). Clearly, teaching strategies to students so that their use becomes second nature requires a great deal of expertise and commitment on the part of teachers. Yet the results are well worth the effort.

Glossary

Alphabetic principle   The concept that letters represent speech sounds.

Ambiguities   Words, phrases, or sentences that are open to more than one interpretation (e.g., *Robber gets 6 months in violin case*).

Anecdotal record   A written account of specific incidents or behaviors in the classroom.

Character motive   An emotion, desire, or need that incites a character into action.

Classwide peer tutoring   Students of different reading abilities are paired together (usually one average or high with one low) to complete a reading task.

Cloze procedure   Words or other structures are deleted from a passage by the teacher, with blanks left in their places for students to fill in; also used as an assessment of reading ability by omitting every *n*th word in a reading passage and observing the number of correct insertions provided by the reader.

Cognitive organizers   Assist students in remembering and following learning strategy procedures; often employ mnemonic devices that cue students to the steps of a strategy.

Collaborative Strategic Reading (CSR)   A multicomponent strategy approach that teaches students to use comprehension strategies while working collaboratively with their peers in small groups.

Comprehension   A person's ability to understand what is being read or discussed.

Computer-assisted instruction (CAI)   Involves learning through the use of computers and/or other multimedia systems.

Context clues   Clues to word meanings or concepts that are found in proceeding or following words or sentences.

Cooperative learning   Students of mixed abilities work together in small groups toward a common academic goal.

Criterion-referenced test   Test designed to measure how well a person has learned information or skills; often uses a cut-off score to determine mastery.

Curriculum-based assessment (CBA)   Assessment used to measure students' progress toward instructional goals and objectives; items are taken from the curriculum, evaluations are repeated frequently over time, and results are used to develop instructional plans.

Curriculum-based measurement (CBM)   A form of CBA that includes a set of standard, simple, short-duration fluency measures of basic skills in reading as well as in other subject areas.

Decoding   Strategy for recognizing words.

Direct instruction   Systematic teacher-directed lessons in specific instructional strategies that usually include a statement of the objective, modeling, scaffolded practice, and error correction.

Elaborative processes   Going beyond the literal meaning of a text to make inferences and connections.

Expository text   Informational or factual text.

Expressions   Include idioms ("hang on"), proverbs ("Don't count your chickens before they've hatched"), slang ("decked out"), catchphrases ("24/7"), and slogans.

Figures of speech   Words that are not used literally but suggest another meaning (e.g., similes, hyperbole).

Fluency   The ability to read accurately and quickly.

Graphic organizer   A visual representation of textual information and ideas.

Hierarchical summary procedure   Technique used to direct students' attention to the organizational structure of passages by previewing, reading, outlining, studying, and retelling.

Informal reading inventory (IRI)   IRIs are individually administered tests that yield information about a student's reading level as well as word analysis and comprehension skills; a student reads lists of words and passages that are leveled by grade and retells or answers comprehension questions about what they read.

Integrative processes   Ability to make connections across sentences by understanding and inferring the relationships among clauses.

Interactive instructional model   Relies on semantic feature analysis using relationship maps and charts and also incorporates interactive strategic dialogues.

Keyword strategies   A memory strategy that assists students in memorizing words or concepts by associating a key word to the concept or word to be remembered.

Learning disability (LD) A neurological disorder that may result in difficulty with reading, writing, spelling, reasoning, recalling, or organizing information; individuals with LD have average or above-average intelligence.

Macroprocessing Involves the ability to summarize and organize key information and to relate smaller units of what has been read to the text as a whole.

Main idea The central message or gist of a small portion of text.

Metacognitive processes Thinking about thinking; the reader's conscious awareness or control of cognitive processes such as monitoring understanding while reading.

Microprocessing Ability to comprehend at the sentence level; chunking idea units to know what is important to remember.

Mnemonic A memory strategy that assists students in memorizing words or concepts (e.g., by associating a key word, image, or rhyme); also called the key word method.

Morphology Using and understanding word formation patterns that include roots, prefixes, suffixes, and inflected endings.

Multicomponent strategy instruction Improves comprehension by teaching a set of strategies to use before, during, and after reading.

Multipass Students make three "passes" through an expository text passage to (1) identify text structure and become familiar with main ideas and organization, (2) read questions at back of chapter and guess at answers, (3) read the text to find the correct answers to the questions.

Narrative text Text that tells a story; generally fiction.

Onomastics The study of names.

Paraphrasing Restating what has been heard or read in your own words; usually more detailed than a summary.

Phonics The association of speech sounds with printed letters; phonics instruction involves using letter–sound correspondences to read and spell words.

Phonological awareness Ability to discriminate between and manipulate speech sounds (e.g., rhyming).

Phonology Discriminating between and producing speech sounds.

Pragmatics Using language to communicate effectively by following generally accepted principles of communication.

Progress monitoring Systematic assessments of students' academic performance that is used to determine what students have learned and to evaluate the effectiveness of instruction.

Question–answer relationships (QAR) strategy A strategy for teaching students how to answer different types of comprehension questions.

Questioning the Author   A strategy to increase comprehension and critical thinking that encourages students to ask questions that focus on the author's intent and choices.

Reader-response theory   Based on the premise that understanding what one reads is related to an individual's experiences and interpretations of these experiences.

Reciprocal teaching   Uses prediction, summarization, question generation, and clarification to guide group discussions of what has been read.

ReQuest procedure   A reading comprehension technique that combines high-quality teacher questions with student-generated questions.

Retelling   Measure of comprehension that asks students to recall and restate the events in a story after they have read it or heard it.

Scaffolding   Instructional technique in which the teacher first models a learning strategy or task, provides learners with appropriate levels of support, and then gradually shifts responsibility to the students until they can perform the task independently.

Schema theory   Existing representations of information influence how new ideas are learned and remembered.

Semantic organizer   A visual representation of information used to facilitate understanding.

Semantics   Understanding word meanings.

Standardized norm-referenced test   Assessment that measures proficiency by comparing an individual's score with with age-level and grade-level peers.

Story grammar   The pattern of elements the reader can expect to find in a narrative text, such as the characters, setting, and plot.

Story maps   Instructional strategy to increase comprehension by creating a graphic representation of a story that includes story elements and how they are connected.

Story structure   The organizational arrangement of written information; when text follows predictable structures it is easier to understand and remember.

Storybook reading   Technique that uses read-alouds specifically to build vocabulary.

Students Achieving Independent Learning (SAIL)   Transactional strategies instruction technique that promotes extensive reading of children's literature and encourages students to set their own purposes and goals for reading and select appropriate comprehension strategies to support their meaning making.

Summarizing   Involves generating multiple main ideas from across the reading and then combining them with important supporting information to form a summary.

Syntax   Using correct phrasing and sentence organization.

TELLS   Comprehension strategy that guides students to (*T*) study story titles, (*E*) examine and skim pages for clues, (*L*) look for important words, (*L*) look for difficult words, and (*S*) think about the story settings.

Text preview   Strategies that are used to activate prior knowledge, make predictions, and engage students before reading.

Text structure   The way a text is organized to guide readers in identifying key information.

Theme   Subject matter, major concept, or topic of a text.

Theme scheme   Technique that provides instruction in different text structure strategies.

Think-aloud   Verbalizing aloud what one is thinking while reading or performing a task.

Transactional strategies instruction   A comprehensive, high-intensity, long-term approach wherein the teacher provides support and guidance to students as they apply comprehension strategies; a goal of instruction is the self-regulated use of strategies.

Vocabulary knowledge   Knowing what words mean in the context in which they are used.

Word analysis   Using letter–sound relationships or other structural patterns (e.g., prefixes) to decode unknown words.

Word associations   Ways to connect words to each other, such as synonyms (*ugly, unattractive*), antonyms (*huge, tiny*), homographs (*desert, desert*), and homophones (*plane, plain*).

Word consciousness   Learning about, playing with, and being interested in words and their many and varied uses.

Word formations   Include acronyms (*USDA*), compounds (*backyard*), and affixes (*neo-, -ing*).

Reading Comprehension Websites

www.ala.org

The website of the American Library Association provides recommendations for books for children, including many suggestions for reluctant and struggling readers.

www.allamericareads.org/

The All America Reads website contains resources and information on reading and reading comprehension. The "Lesson Plans" section provides suggestions for before, during, and after reading strategies, as well as vocabulary acquisition strategies.

cars.uth.tmc.edu

The website for the Center for Academic and Reading Skills at the University of Texas–Houston Health Science Center and the University of Houston provides resources on the assessment and teaching of reading.

www.ciera.org

The Center for Improvement of Early Reading Achievement (CIERA) website provides resources for teaching early reading. The link to the CIERA Archive contains key publications in early literacy for teachers and researchers.

curry.edschool.virginia.edu/go/readquest/strat/

The Reading Quest website focuses on teaching social studies and provides links to reading comprehension resources and strategies that can be used in a variety of subject areas (most include black-line masters and handouts).

www.ed.gov/

The website for the U.S. Department of Education provides research, statistics, information, and resources on education. The "Teaching Resources" section contains links and publications on teaching reading comprehension, literature, and vocabulary.

www.interdys.org

The International Dyslexia Association website provides resources for teaching individuals with reading disabilities.

www.ldonline.org/

The Learning Disabilities Online website provides information and resources on teaching, research, and reading disabilities and other disabilities. It also includes resources for parents and students.

www.ldresources.com/

The Learning Disabilities Resources website provides a large number of entries on all aspects of learning to read and a forum for comments and feedback on these topics.

www.literacy.uconn.edu/compre.htm

The reading comprehension section of the University of Connecticut Literacy Web provides a wealth of resources on comprehension instruction, vocabulary instruction, strategies, and activities, including resources for teaching English language learners.

www.NationalReadingPanel.org

The National Reading Panel website provides a current review of the research on teaching reading.

www.ncld.org

The website for the National Center for Learning Disabilities provides information and resources related to learning disabilities, including reading disabilities. The "LD InfoZone" link provides syntheses of research in various areas of reading, including reading comprehension.

www.ncte.org

The website for the National Council of Teachers of English includes numerous resources on teaching literature and children's literature.

reading.uoregon.edu

The Reading website provides useful links to information on reading comprehension and other areas of reading. The "Big Ideas" link contains resources on the five key elements of beginning reading, including critical features of comprehension instruction.

www.reading.org

The International Reading Association website provides a host of resources on teaching reading. The comprehension section has books, articles, position statements, and links to online resources. Teachers may also find useful the lesson plans, booklists, and parent resources.

www.readingrockets.org/

This website for Reading Rockets provides research findings on effective reading instruction. The site also contains links to information and resources on reading comprehension, professional development opportunities (e.g., "Comprehension: Helping ELLs grasp the full picture"), and effective teaching strategies.

www.readwritethink.org/

The Read Write Think website provides a variety of reading information, including lessons, standards, resources, and student materials. The "Learning about Language" link contains reading comprehension information.

www.studentprogress.org/

The National Center on Student Progress Monitoring website provides information about progress monitoring to assess students' academic performance and evaluate the effectiveness of instruction in reading.

www.successforall.net

The Success for All website provides information about the Success for All Program, including effective practice research.

www.texas.org

The website for the Texas Center for Reading and Language Arts at the University of Texas at Austin provides a wide range of resources and materials to download for teaching reading.

References

Alfassi, M. (1998). Reading for meaning: The efficacy of reciprocal teaching in fostering reading comprehension in high school students in remedial classes. *American Educational Research Journal, 35,* 309–332.

Allen, J. (1999). *Word, words, words: Teaching vocabulary in grades 4–12.* Portland, ME: Stenhouse.

Amer, A. A. (1992). The effect of story grammar instruction on EFL students' comprehension of narrative text. *Reading in a Foreign Language, 8*(2), 711–720.

Anderson, R. C., Hiebert, E. H., Scott, J. A., & Wilkinson, I. (1985). *Becoming a nation of readers.* Washington, DC: National Institute of Education.

Anderson, R. C., & Nagy, W. E. (1992). The vocabulary conundrum. *American Educator, 16,* 14–18, 44–47.

Anderson, R. C., & Pearson, P. D. (1984). A schema-theoretic view of basic processes in reading comprehension. In P. D. Pearson, R. Barr, M. L. Kamil, & P. Mosenthal (Eds.), *Handbook of reading research* (Vol. 1, pp. 255–292). White Plains, NY: Longman.

Anderson, V. (1992). A teacher development project in transactional strategy instruction for teachers of severely reading-disabled adolescents. *Teaching and Teacher Education, 8,* 391–403.

Applegate, M. D., Quinn, K. B., & Applegate, A. J. (2002). Levels of thinking required by comprehension questions in Informal Reading Inventories. *Reading Teacher, 56*(2), 174–180.

Armbruster, B. B., & Anderson, T. H. (1981). *Content area textbooks.* Reading Report No. 23. Champaign, IL: University of Illinois, Center for the Study of Reading.

Armbruster, B. B., Anderson, T. H., & Ostertag, J. (1987). Does text structure/summarization instruction facilitate learning from expository text? *Reading Research Quarterly, 22,* 331–346.

Bader, A. L. (1998). *Bader Reading and Language Inventory—Third Edition.* Upper Saddle River, NJ: Prentice Hall.

Baker, L. (2002). Metacognition in strategy instruction. In C. C. Block & M. Pressley (Eds.), *Comprehension instruction: Research-based best practices* (pp. 77–95). New York: Guilford Press.

Baker, S., Gersten, R., & Graham, S. (2003). Teaching expressive writing to students with learning disabilities: Research-based applications and examples. *Journal of Learning Disabilities, 36*(2), 109–123.

Bakken, J. P., & Whedon, C. K. (2002). Teaching text structure to improve reading comprehension. *Intervention in School and Clinic, 37*, 229–233.

Ball, E. W., & Blachman, B. A. (1991). Does phoneme awareness training in kindergarten make a difference in early word recognition and developmental spelling? *Reading Research Quarterly, 26*, 49–66.

Bauman, J., & Kame'enui, E. (1991). Research on vocabulary instruction: Ode to Voltaire. In J. Flood, J. Jensen, D. Lapp, & J. Squire (Eds.). *Handbook on teaching the English language arts* (pp. 604–632). New York: Macmillan.

Baumann, J. F. (1984). The effectiveness of a direct instruction paradigm for teaching main idea comprehension. *Reading Research Quarterly, 20*, 93–115.

Baumann, J. F., Edwards, E. C., Boland, E. M., Olejnik, S., & Kame'enui, E. J. (2003). Vocabulary tricks: Effects of instruction in morphology and context on fifth-grade students' ability to derive and infer word meanings. *American Educational Research Journal, 40*(2), 447–494.

Beach, R. (1993). *A teachers' introduction to reader response theories.* Urbana, IL: National Council of Teachers of English.

Bean, T. W., Potter, T. C., & Clark, C. (1980). Selected semantic features of ESL materials and their effect on bilingual students' comprehension. In M. Kamil & A. Moe (Eds.), *Perspectives on reading research and instruction: Twenty-ninth yearbook of the National Reading Conference* (pp. 1–5). Washington, DC: National Reading Conference.

Beaver, J. (1997). *Developmental Reading Assessment* (DRA). Lebanon, IN: Pearson Learning Group.

Beck, I. L. (2006). *Making sense of phonics: The hows and whys.* New York: Guilford Press.

Beck, I. L., & McKeown, M. G. (1983). A program to enhance vocabulary and comprehension. *The Reading Teacher, 36*, 622–625.

Beck, I. L., & McKeown, M. G. (1998). Comprehension: The sine qua non of reading. In S. Patton & M. Holmes (Eds.), *The keys to literacy* (pp. 40–52). Washington, DC: Council for Basic Education.

Beck, I. L., McKeown, M. G., & Kucan, L. (2002). *Bringing words to life: Robust vocabulary instruction.* New York: Guilford Press.

Beck, I. L., McKeown, M. G., & Omanson, R. C. (1987). The effects and uses of diverse vocabulary instructional techniques. In M. G. McKeown & M. E. Curtis (Eds.), *The nature of vocabulary acquisition* (pp. 147–163). Hillsdale, NJ: Erlbaum.

Beck, I. L., McKeown, M. G., Omanson, R. C., & Pople, M. T. (1985). Some effects of the nature and frequency of vocabulary instruction on the knowledge and use of words. *Reading Research Quarterly, 20*, 522–535.

Beck, I. L., McKeown, M. G., Sandora, C., Kucan, L., & Worthy, J. (1996). Questioning the author: A yearlong classroom implementation to engage students with text. *Elementary School Journal, 96*(4), 385–414.

Bell, R. Q. (1968). A reinterpretation of the direction of effects in studies of socialization. *Psychological Review, 75*, 81–95.

Bergman, J. L. (1992). SAIL: A way to success and independence for low-achieving readers. *The Reading Teacher, 45*, 598–602.

Berry, G., Hall, D., & Gildroy, P. G. (2004). Teaching learning strategies. In K. Lenz, D. Deshler, & B. R. Kissam (Eds.), *Teaching content to all: Evidence-based inclusive practices in middle and secondary schools* (pp. 258–278). Boston: Pearson Education.

Bintz, W. (2000). Using freewriting to assess reading comprehension. *Reading Horizons, 40*(3), 205–222.

Blachowicz, C. L. Z., & Fisher, P. (2004). Keep the "fun" in fundamental: Encouraging word awareness and incidental word learning in the classroom through word play. In J. F. Baumann & E. J. Kame'enui (Eds.), *Vocabulary instruction: Research to practice* (pp. 218–238). New York: Guilford Press.

Blachowicz, C., & Ogle, D. (2001). *Reading comprehension: Strategies for independent learners.* New York: Guilford Press.

Blanton, W. E., Wood, K. D., & Moorman, G. B. (1990). The role of purpose in reading instruction. *The Reading Teacher, 43*, 486–493.

Bos, C. S. (1987). *Promoting story comprehension using a story retelling strategy.* Paper presented at the Teachers Applying Whole Language Conference, Tucson, AZ.

Bos, C. S., & Anders, P. L. (1992). Using interactive teaching and learning strategies to promote text comprehension and content learning for students with learning disabilities. *International Journal of Disability, Development and Education, 39*, 225–238.

Bos, C. S., & Vaughn, S. (2002). *Strategies for teaching students with learning and behavior problems* (5th ed.). Boston: Allyn & Bacon.

Boyle, J. R., & Weishaar, M. (1997). The effects of expert-generated versus student-generated cognitive organizers on the reading comprehension of students with learning disabilities. *Learning Disabilities Research and Practice, 12*(4), 228–235.

Brand-Gruwal, S., Aarnoutse, C. A. J., & Van Den Bos, K. P. (1997). Improving text comprehension strategies in reading and listening settings. *Learning and Instruction, 8*(1), 63–81.

Bransford, J., Brown, A. L., & Cocking, R. R. (1999). *How people learn: Brain, mind, experience, and school.* Washington, DC: Committee on Developments in the Science of Learning, National Research Council.

Brown, A. L., & Campione, J. C. (1996). Theory and design of learning environments. In L. Schauble & R. Glaser (Eds.), *Innovations in learning: New environments for education* (pp. 289–325). Mahwah, NJ: Erlbaum.

Brown, A. L., & Day, J. D. (1983). Macrorules for summarizing texts: The development of expertise. *Journal of Verbal Learning and Verbal Behavior, 22*(1), 1–14.

Brown, A. L., & Palincsar, A. S. (1989). Guided, cooperative learning and individual knowledge acquisition. In L. B. Resnick (Ed.), *Knowing, learning, and instruction: Essays in honor of Robert Glaser* (pp. 393–451). Hillsdale, NJ: Erlbaum.

Brown, L. V., Hammill, D. D., & Wiederholt, J. L. (1995). *The Test of Reading Comprehension— Third Edition* (TORC-3). Circle Pines, MN: AGS.

Brown, R., Pressley, M., Van Meter, P., & Schuder, T. (1996). A quasi-experimental validation of transactional strategies instruction with low-achieving second grade readers. *Journal of Educational Psychology, 88*, 18–37.

Bryant, D. P., Goodwin, M., Bryant, B. R., & Higgins, K. (2003). Vocabulary instruction for students with learning disabilities: A review of the research. *Learning Disability Quarterly, 26*, 117–128.

Bryant, D. P., Vaughn, S., Linan-Thompson, S., Ugel, N., & Hamff, A. (2000). Reading outcomes for students with and without learning disabilities in general education middle school content area classes. *Learning Disability Quarterly, 23*(3), 24–38.

Cain, K. (1996). Story knowledge and comprehension skill. In C. Cornoldi & J. V. Oakhill

(Eds.), *Reading comprehension difficulties: Processes and remediation* (pp. 167–192). Mahwah, NJ: Erlbaum.

Carrell, P. L. (1984). Evidence of a formal schema in second language comprehension. *Language Learning, 34*(2) 87–112.

Carrell, P. L. (1992). Awareness of text structure: Effects on recall. *Language Learning, 42*(1), 1–20.

Casteel, C. P., Isom, B. A., & Jordan, K. F. (2000). Creating confident and competent readers: Transactional strategies instruction. *Intervention in School and Clinic, 36,* 67–74.

Cazden, C. (1988). *Classroom discourse: The language of teaching and learning.* Portsmouth, NH: Heinemann.

Champion, A. (1997). Knowledge of suffixed words: A comparison of reading disabled and nondisabled readers. *Annals of Dyslexia, 47,* 29–55.

Chang, J., & Shimizu, W. (1997, January). *Collaborative strategic reading: Cross-age and cross-cultural applications.* Paper presented at the Council for Exceptional Children Symposium on Culturally and Linguistically Diverse Exceptional Learners, New Orleans, LA.

Chen, H., & Graves, M. F. (1995). Effects of previewing and providing background knowledge on Taiwanese college students comprehension of American short stories. *TESOL Quarterly, 29*(4), 663–686.

Ciardiello, A. V. (2002). Helping adolescents understand cause/effect text structure in social studies. *Social Studies, 93*(1), 31–36.

Collins, C. (1991). Reading instruction that increases thinking abilities. *Journal of Reading, 34,* 510–516.

Cunningham, A. E., & Stanovich, K. E. (1991). Tracking the unique effects of print exposure in children: Associations with vocabulary, general knowledge, and spelling. *Journal of Educational Psychology, 83,* 264–274.

Cunningham, J. W., & Wall, L. (1994). Teaching good readers to comprehend better. *Journal of Reading, 37,* 480–486.

Dale, E. (1965). Vocabulary measurement: Techniques and major findings. *Elementary English, 42,* 82–88.

Darch, C., & Gersten, R. (1986). Direction-setting activities in reading comprehension: A comparison of two approaches. *Learning Disability Quarterly, 9,* 235–243.

Darch, C., & Kame'enui, E. J. (1987). Teaching LD students critical reading skills: A systematic replication. *Learning Disability Quarterly, 10,* 82–91.

Deno, S. L. (1985). Curriculum-based measurement: The emerging alternative. *Exceptional Children, 52,* 219–232.

Deno, S. (1992). The nature and development of curriculum-based measurement. *Preventing School Failure, 36,* 5–10.

Dewitz, P., & Dewitz, P. K. (2003). They can read the words, but they can't understand: Refining comprehension assessment. *Reading Teacher, 56*(5), 422–435.

Dickson, S. (1999). Integrating reading and writing to teach compare–contrast text structure: A research-based methodology. *Reading and Writing Quarterly, 14,* 49–79.

Dickson, S. V., Simmons, D., & Kame'enui, E. J. (1995). Instruction in expository text: A focus on compare–contrast structure. *LD Forum, 20*(2), 8–15.

Dole, J. A., Duffy, G. G., Roehler, L. R., & Pearson, P. D. (1991). Moving from the old to the new: Research on reading comprehension instruction. *Review of Educational Research, 61,* 239–264.

Dole, J. A., Valencia, S. W., Greer, E. A., & Wardrop, J. L. (1991). Effects of two types of prereading instruction on the comprehension of narrative and expository text. *Reading Research Quarterly, 26*(2), 142–159.

Duke, N. K., & Pearson, D. (2002). Effective practices for developing reading comprehension. In A. E. Farstrup & S. J. Samuels (Eds.), *What research has to say about reading instruction* (3rd ed., pp. 205–242). Newark, DE: International Reading Association.

Durkin, D. (1978–1979). What classroom observations reveal about reading comprehension instruction. *Reading Research Quarterly, 14,* 481–533.

Einstein, A. (1961). *Relativity: The special and the general theory* (R. W. Lawson, Trans.). New York: Bonanza Books.

El-Dinary, P. B., Pressley, M., & Schuder, T. (1992). Teachers learning transactional strategies instruction. In C. K. Kinzer & D. J. Leu (Eds.), *Literacy research, theory, and practice: Views from many perspectives: 41st yearbook of the National Reading Conference* (pp. 453–462). Chicago: National Reading Conference.

Ellis, E. S., & Farmer, T. (2005). The clarifying routine: Elaborating vocabulary instruction. Retrieved March 3, 2006, from *www.ldonline.org*

Englert, C. S. (1990). Unraveling the mysteries of writing through strategy instruction. In T. Scruggs & B. Wong (Eds.), *Intervention research in learning disabilities* (pp. 186–223). New York: Springer-Verlag.

Englert, C. S. (1992). Writing instruction from a sociocultural perspective: The holistic, dialogic, and social enterprise of writing. *Journal of Learning Disabilities, 25,* 153–172.

Englert, C. S., & Hiebert, E. H. (1984). Children's developing awareness of text structures in expository materials. *Journal of Education Psychology, 76,* 65–75.

Englert, C. S., Garmon, A., Mariage, T., Rozendal, M., Tarrant, K., & Urba, J. (1995). The early literacy project: Connecting across the literacy curriculum. *Learning Disability Quarterly, 18,* 253–275.

Espin, C. A., Shin, J., & Busch, T. W. (2005). Curriculum-based measurement in the content areas: Vocabulary matching as an indicator of progress in social studies learning. *Journal of Learning Disabilities, 38*(4), 353–363.

Fillmore, L. W., & Snow, C. (2000). *What teachers need to know about language.* Available at *www.cal.org/resources/teachers.pdf*

Fitzgerald, J. (1995). English-as-a-second-language learners' cognitive reading processes: A review of research in the United States. *Review of Educational Research, 65,* 145–190.

Flavell, J. H. (1979). Metacognition and cognitive monitoring: A new area of cognitive–developmental inquiry. *American Psychologist, 34,* 906–911.

Flynt, E. S., & Cooter, R., Jr. (1998). *Flynt–Cooter Reading Inventory for the Classroom.* Columbus, OH: Merrill Education (Prentice Hall).

Fuchs, D., Fuchs, L. S., Mathes, P. G., & Lipsey, M. W. (2000). Reading differences between low-achieving students with and without learning disabilities: A meta-analysis. In R. Gersten, E. P. Schiller, & S. Vaughn (Eds.), *Contemporary special education research: Syntheses of the knowledge base on critical instruction issues* (pp. 81–105). Mahwah, NJ: Erlbaum.

Fuchs, D., Fuchs, L. S., Mathes, P. G., & Simmons, D. C. (1997). Peer assisted learning strategies: Making classrooms more responsive to diversity. *American Educational Research Journal, 34,* 174–206.

Fuchs, L., & Deno, S. (1992). Effects of curriculum within curriculum-based measurement. *Exceptional Children, 58,* 232–243.

Fuchs, L. S., & Fuchs, D. (1999). Monitoring student progress toward the development of reading competence: A review of three forms of classroom-based assessment. *School Pyschology Review, 28*(4), 659–671.

Fuchs, L. S., & Fuchs, D. (2003). Curriculum-Based Measurement: A best practice guide. *NASP Communique, 32*(2).

Fuchs, L. S., Fuchs, D., Hamlett, C., Philips, N., & Bentz, J. (1994). Classwide curriculum-based measurement: Helping general educators meet the challenge of student diversity. *Exceptional Children, 60,* 15–24.

Gajria, M., & Salvia, J. (1992). The effects of summarization instruction on text comprehension of students with learning disabilities. *Exceptional Children, 58*(6), 508–516.

Gall, M. (1984). Synthesis of research on teachers' questioning. *Educational Leadership, 42*(3), 40–47.

Garner, R. (1992). Metacognition and self-monitoring strategies. In S. J. Samuels & A. E. Farstrup (Eds.), *What research has to say about reading instruction.* (2nd ed., pp. 236–252). Newark, DE: International Reading Association.

Gaskins, I. W., Anderson, R. C., Pressley, M., Cunicelli, E. A., & Satlow, E. (1993). Six teachers' dialogue during cognitive process instruction. *Elementary School Journal, 93,* 277–304.

Geisel, T. S. (1971). *The Lorax by Dr. Suess.* New York: Random House.

Gersten, R., Fuchs, L., Williams, J. P., & Baker, S. (2001). Teaching reading comprehension strategies to students with learning disabilities: A review of research. *Review of Educational Research, 71,* 279–320.

Gersten, R., Fuchs, L., Williams, J., & Baker, S. (2001). Teaching reading comprehension strategies to students with learning disabilities: A review of research. *Review of Educational Research, 71,* 279–320.

Gillis, M. K., & Olson, M. W. (1987). Elementary IRIs: Do they reflect what we know about text type/structure and comprehension? *Reading Research and Instruction, 27,* 36–44.

Goldman, S. R., & Rakestraw, J. A. (2000). Structural aspects of constructing meaning from text. In M. L. Kamil, P. B. Mosenthal, P. D. Pearson, & R. Barr (Eds.), *Handbook of reading research* (Vol. 3, pp. 311–335). Mahwah, NJ: Erlbaum.

Goldstone, B. P. (2002). Whaz up with our books? Changing picture book codes and teaching implications. *The Reading Teacher, 55,* 362–370.

Graves, A. W. (1986). Effects of direct instruction and metacomprehension training on finding main ideas. *Learning Disabilities Research, 1,* 90–100.

Graves, M. F. (2000). A vocabulary program to complement and bolster a middle-grade comprehension program. In B. M. Taylor, M. F. Graves, & P. van den Broek (Eds.), *Reading for meaning: Fostering comprehension in the middle grades* (pp. 116–135). Newark, DE: International Reading Association.

Graves, M. F. (2004). Teaching prefixes: As good as it gets? In J. F. Baumann & E. J. Kame'enui (Eds.), *Vocabulary instruction: Research to practice* (pp. 81–99). New York: Guilford Press.

Graves, M. F., Brunetti, G. J., & Slater, W. H. (1982). The reading vocabularies of primary-grade children of varying geographic and social backgrounds. In J. A. Harris & L. A. Harris (Eds.), *New inquiries in reading research and instruction* (pp. 99–104). Rochester, NY: National Reading Conference.

Graves, M. F., Calfee, R., Graves, B. B., & Juel, C. (2006). *Teaching reading in the 21st century* (4th ed.). Boston: Allyn & Bacon.

Graves, M. F., Juel, C., & Graves, B. B. (2001). *Teaching reading in the 21st century* (2nd ed.). Boston: Allyn & Bacon.

Graves, M. F., Prenn, M., & Cooke, C. L. (1985). The coming attractions: Previewing short stories. *Journal of Reading, 28*(7), 594–598.

Gunning, T. G. (2002). *Assessing and correcting reading and writing difficulties* (2nd ed.). Boston: Allyn & Bacon.

Haager, D., & Klingner, J. K. (2005). *Differentiating instruction in inclusive classrooms: The special educators' guide.* Boston: Allyn & Bacon.

Hansen, C. L. (1978). Story retelling used with average and learning disabled readers as a measure of reading comprehension. *Learning Disability Quarterly,1,* 62–69.

Harcourt Assessment. (2002). *Stanford 10 Reading Assessment.* San Antonio, TX: Author.

Harcourt, Brace Educational Measurement. (1996). *Key Links: The Difference between Instruction and Assessment.* San Antonio, TX: Author.

Harniss, M. K., Dickson, S. V., Kinder, D., & Hollenbeck, K. L. (2001). Textual problems and instructional solutions: Strategies for enhancing learning from published history textbooks. *Reading and Writing Quarterly: Overcoming Learning Difficulties, 17,* 127–150.

Harris, K. R., & Graham, S. (1999). Programmatic intervention research: Illustrations from the evolution of self-regulated strategy development. *Learning Disability Quarterly, 22,* 251–262.

Hasbrouck, J. E., & Tindal, G. (1992). Curriculum-based oral reading fluency norms for students in grades 2 through 4. *Teaching Exceptional Children, 24*(3), 41–44.

Hawkins, G. S. (1983). *Mindsteps to the cosmos.* New York: Harper & Row.

Heilman, A. W., Blair, T.R., & Rupley, W. H. (1998). *Principles and practices of teaching reading* (9th ed.). Columbus, OH: Merrill/Prentice Hall.

Hickman, P., Pollard-Durodola, S., & Vaughn, S. (2004). Storybook reading: Improving vocabulary and comprehension for English language learners. *Reading Teacher, 57*(8), 720–730.

Hinds, J. (1983). Contrastive rhetoric: Japanese and English. *Text, 3*(2), 183–195.

Hirsch, E. D., Jr. (2003). Reading comprehension requires word knowledge—of words and the world: Scientific insights into the fourth grade slump and the nation's stagnant comprehension scores. *American Educator, 27*(1), 10–13.

Hoover, H. D., Hieronymus, A. N., Frisbie, D. A., & Dunbar, S. B. (1996). *Iowa Test of Basic Skills* (ITBS). Itasca, IL: Riverside.

Hutchins, E. (1991). The social organization of distributed cognition. In L. Resnick, J. M. Levine, & S. D. Teasley (Eds.), *Perspectives on socially shared cognition* (pp. 283–307). Washington, DC: American Psychological Association.

Idol, L. (1987). Group story mapping: A comprehension strategy for both skilled and unskilled readers. *Journal of Learning Disabilities, 20,* 196–205.

Idol-Maestas, L. (1985). Getting ready to read: Guided probing for poor comprehenders. *Learning Disability Quarterly, 8,* 243–254.

Invernizz, M.A., & Abouzeid, M. P. (1995). One story map does not fit all: A cross cultural analysis of children's written story retellings. *Journal of Narrative and Life History, 5,* 1–19.

Irwin, J. W. (1991). *Teaching reading comprehension processes* (2nd ed.). Englewood Cliffs, NJ: Prentice Hall.

Irwin, J. W., & Baker, I. (1989). *Promoting active reading strategies.* Englewood Cliffs, NJ: Prentice Hall.

Jenkins, J. R., Heliotis, J., Stein, M. L., & Haynes, M. (1987). Improving reading comprehension by using paragraph restatements. *Exceptional Children, 54,* 54–59.

Jenkins, J. R., Larson, K., & Fleisher, L. S. (1983). Effects of error correction on word recognition and reading comprehension. *Learning Disability Quarterly, 6,* 139–145.

Jiménez, R. T., Garcia, G. E., & Pearson, P. D. (1995). Three children, two languages, and strategic reading: Case studies in bilingual/monolingual reading. *American Educational Research Journal, 32,* 67–97.

Jiménez, R. T., Garcia, G. E., & Pearson, P. D. (1996). The reading strategies of bilingual Latino students who are successful English readers: Opportunities and obstacles. *Reading Research Quarterly, 31,* 90–112.

Jitendra, A. K., Cole, C. L., Hoppes, M. K., & Wilson, B. (1998). Effects of a direct instruction main idea summarization program and self-monitoring on reading comprehension of middle school students with learning disabilities. *Reading and Writing Quarterly: Overcoming Learning Difficulties, 14*(4), 379–396.

Jitendra, A. K., Edwards, L. L., Sacks, G., & Jacobson, L. A. (2004). What research says about vocabulary instruction for students with learning disabilities. *Exceptional Children, 70*(3), 299–322.

Jitendra, A. K., Hoppes, M. K., & Xin, Y. P. (2000). Enhancing main idea comprehension for students with learning problems: The role of a summarization strategy and self-monitoring instruction. *Journal of Special Education, 34*(3), 127–139.

Jitendra, A. K., Nolet, V., Xin, Y. P., Gomez, O., Renouf, K., & Iskold, L. (2001). An analysis of middle school geography textbooks: Implications for students with learning problems. *Reading and Writing Quarterly, 17,* 151–173.

Johnson, D. D., Johnson, B. V. H., & Schlichting, K. (2004). Logology: Word and language play. In J. F. Baumann & E. J. Kame'enui (Eds.), *Vocabulary instruction: Research to practice* (pp. 179–200). New York: Guilford Press.

Johnson, D. W., & Johnson, R. T. (1989). Cooperative learning: What special educators need to know. *The Pointer, 33,* 5–10.

Johnson-Glenberg, M. C. (2000). Training reading comprehension in adequate decoders/poor comprehenders: Verbal versus visual strategies. *Journal of Educational Psychology, 92*(4), 772–782.

Kagan, S. (1991). *Cooperative learning.* San Diego: Kagan Cooperative Learning.

Kaiser, E. (1997). Story retelling: Linking assessment to the teaching–learning cycle. *Weaving Authentic Assessment into the Tapestry of Learning, 2*(1). Retrieved June 29, 2006, from http://ccvi.wceruw.org/ccvi/zz-pubs/newsletters/winter1997_weavingauthenticassessment/Story_Retelling_V2_No1.html

Kamhi, A. G. (1997). Three perspectives on comprehension: Implications for assessing and treating comprehension problems. *Topics in Language Disorders, 17*(3), 62–74.

Kamil, M. L. (2004). Vocabulary and comprehension instruction: Summary and implications of the National Reading Panel Findings. In P. McCardle & V. Chhabra (Eds.), *The voice of evidence in reading research* (pp. 213–234). Baltimore: Brookes.

Kaufman, A., & Kaufman, N. (1998). *Kaufman Test of Educational Achievment* (K-TEA-R/NU). Circle Pines, MN: American Guidance Service.

Keene, E. O., & Zimmermann, S. (1997). *Mosaic of thought: Teaching comprehension in a reader's workshop.* Portsmouth, NH: Heinemann.

Kim, A., Vaughn, S., Klingner, J. K., Woodruff, A. L., Klein, C., & Kouzekanani, K. (2006). Improving the reading comprehension of middle school students with disabilities through computer-assisted collaborative strategic reading (CACSR). *Remedial and Special Education, 27,* 235–248.

King, C. M., & Parent Johnson, L. M. (1999). Constructing meaning via reciprocal teaching. *Reading Research and Instruction, 38*(3), 169–186.

King-Sears, M. E. (1994). *Curriculum-based assessment in special education.* San Diego: Singular.

Kintsch, W., & Greene, E. (1978). The role of culture-specific schemata in the comprehension and recall of stories. *Discourse Processes, 1,* 1–13.

Klingner, J. K. (2004). Assessing reading comprehension. *Assessment for Effective Instruction* (formerly *Diagnostique*), *29*(4), 59–70.

Klingner, J. K., Sturges, K., & Harry, B. (2003). Conducting ethnographic classroom observations of literacy instruction. In S. Vaughn & K. Briggs (Eds.), *Reading in the classroom: Systems for observing teaching and learning.* Baltimore: Brookes.

Klingner, J. K., & Vaughn, S. (1996). Reciprocal teaching of reading comprehension strategies for students with learning disabilities who use English as a second language. *Elementary School Journal, 96,* 275–293.

Klingner, J. K., & Vaughn, S. (1999). Promoting reading comprehension, content learning, and English acquisition through collaborative strategic reading (CSR). *The Reading Teacher, 52,* 738–747.

Klingner, J. K., & Vaughn, S. (2000). The helping behaviors of fifth-graders while using collaborative strategic reading (CSR) during ESL content classes. *TESOL Quarterly, 34,* 69–98.

Klingner, J. K., Vaughn, S., Argüelles, M. E., Hughes, M. T., & Ahwee, S. (2004). Collaborative strategic reading: "Real world" lessons from classroom teachers. *Remedial and Special Education, 25,* 291–302.

Klingner, J. K., Vaughn, S., Dimino, J., Schumm, J. S., & Bryant, D. (2001). *Collaborative strategic reading: Strategies for improving comprehension.* Longmont, CO: Sopris West.

Klingner, J. K., Vaughn, S., & Schumm, J. S. (1998). Collaborative strategic reading during social studies in heterogeneous fourth-grade classrooms. *Elementary School Journal, 99,* 3–21.

Kukan, L., & Beck, I. L. (1997). Thinking aloud and reading comprehension research: Inquiry, instruction, and social interaction. *Review of Educational Research, 67,* 271–299.

Lee, S., Basu, S., Tyler, C. W., & Wei, I. W. (2004). Ciliate populations as bio-indicators at a Deer Island treatment plant. *Advances in Environmental Research, 8*(3–4), 371–378.

Lipson, M. Y., Mosenthal, J. H., & Mekkelsen, J. (1999). The nature of comprehension among grade 2 children: Variability in retellings as a function of development, text, and task. In T. Shanahan & F. Rodriguez-Brown (Ed.), *National reading conference yearbook 48.* Chicago: National Reading Conference.

Lloyd, J., Cullinan, D., Heins, E. D., & Epstein, M. H. (1980). Direct instruction: Effects on oral and written language comprehension. *Learning Disability Quarterly, 3,* 70–77.

Lorio, N. (2006). Up in smoke. *Time Magazine for Kids, 11*(22). Available at *www.timeforkids. com/TFK/magazines/story/0,6277,1177200,00.html.*

Lysynchuk, L. M., Pressley, M., & Vye, N. J. (1990). Reciprocal teaching improves standardized reading-comprehension performance in poor comprehenders. *Elementary School Journal, 90*(5), 469–484.

MacArthur, C. A., Graham, S., Schwartz, S. S., & Schafer, W. (1995). Evaluation of a writing instruction model that integrated a process approach, strategy instruction, and word processing. *Learning Disability Quarterly, 18,* 278–291.

MacArthur, C. A., Schwartz, S. S., & Graham, S. (1991). Effects of a reciprocal peer revision strategy in special education classrooms. *Learning Disabilities Research and Practice, 12,* 16–28.

MacGinitie, W. H., MacGinitie, R. K., Maria, K., & Dreyer, L. G. (2000). *Gates–MacGinitie Reading Tests—Fourth Edition.* Itasca, IL: Riverside.

Malone, L. D., & Mastropieri, M. (1992). Reading comprehension instruction: Summarization and self-monitoring training for students with learning disabilities. *Exceptional Children, 58*(3), 270–279.

Mandler, J. M., & DeForest, M. (1979). Is there more than one way to recall a story? *Child Development, 50*, 886–889.

Mandler, J. M., & Johnson, N. S. (1977). Remembrance of things parsed: Story structure and recall. *Cognitive Psychology, 9*, 111–151.

Manzo, A. V. (1968). *Improving reading comprehension through reciprocal questioning.* Unpublished doctoral dissertation, Syracuse University, Syracuse, NY.

Manzo, A. V., & Manzo, U. C. (1993). *Literacy disorders: Holistic diagnosis and remediation.* Fort Worth, TX: Harcourt Brace Jovanovich.

Markman, E. M. (1985). Comprehension monitoring: Developmental and educational issues. In S. F. Chapman, J. W. Segal, & R. Glaser (Eds.), *Thinking and learning skills: Research and open questions* (pp. 275–291). Mahwah, NJ: Erlbaum.

Marston, D., & Magnusson, D. (1985). Implementing curriculum-based measurement in special and regular education settings. *Exceptional Children, 52*, 266–276.

Marston, D., Deno, S. L., Kim, D., Diment, K., & Rogers, D. (1995). Comparison of reading intervention approaches for students with mild disabilities. *Exceptional Children, 62*, 20–37.

Mastropieri, M. A., & Scruggs, T. E. (1997). Best practices in promoting reading comprehension in students with learning disabilities: 1976 to 1996. *Remedial and Special Education, 18*(4), 197–214.

Mastropieri, M. A., & Scruggs, T. E. (1998). Enhancing school success with mnemonic strategies. *Intervention in School and Clinic, 33*(4), 201–208.

Mastropieri, M. A., Scruggs, T. E., Bakken, J. P., & Whedon, C. (1996). Reading comprehension: A synthesis of research in learning disabilities. In T. E. Scruggs & M. A. Mastropieri (Eds.), *Advances in learning and behavioral disabilities* (pp. 277–303). Greenwich, CT: JAI Press.

McCabe, A. (1995). *Chameleon readers: Teaching children to appreciate all kinds of good stories.* New York: McGraw-Hill.

McClure, E., Mason, J., & Williams, J. (1983). Sociocultural variables in children's sequence of stories. *Discourse Processes, 6*, 131–143.

McCormick, S. (1999). *Instructing students who have literacy problems* (3rd ed.). Upper Saddle River, NJ: Merrill.

McGee, L. M., & Richgels, D. J. (1985). Teaching expository text structure to elementary students. *The Reading Teacher, 38*, 739–748.

McIntosh, R., Vaughn, S., Schumm, J., Haager, D., & Lee, O. (1993). Observations of students with learning disabilities in general education classrooms. *Exceptional Children, 60*(3), 249–261.

McKeown, M. G., & Beck, I. L. (2004). Transforming knowledge into professional development resources: Six teachers implement a model of teaching for understanding text. *Elementary School Journal, 104*, 391–408.

McKeown, M. G., Beck, I. L., Omanson, R. C., & Pople, M. T. (1985). Some effects of the nature and frequency of vocabulary instruction on the knowledge of use of words. *Reading Research Quarterly, 20*(5), 522–535.

Meyer, B. J. F. (1984). Text dimensions and cognitive processing. In H. Mandl, N. Stein, & T. Trabasso (Eds.), *Learning and understanding texts* (pp. 3–47). Hillsdale, NJ: Erlbaum.

Meyer, B. J. F. (2003). Text coherence and readability. *Topics in Language Disorders, 23*(3), 204–224.

Meyer, B., Brandt, D., & Bluth, G. (1980). Use of top-level structure in text: Key for reading comprehension of ninth-grade students. *Reading Research Quarterly, 16,* 72–103.

Michaels, S. (1981). "Sharing time": Children's narrative styles and differential access to literacy. *Language in Society, 10,* 423–442.

Mokhtari, K., & Reichard, C. A. (2002). Assessing students' metacognitive awareness of reading strategies. *Journal of Educational Psychology, 94,* 249–259.

Monti, D., & Ciccheti, G. (1996). *TARA: Think aloud reading assessment.* Austin, TX: Steck-Vaughn Berrent.

Morrow, L. M. (1986). Effects of structural guidance in story retelling on children's dictation of original stories. *Journal of Reading Behavior, 18,* 135–152.

National Institute of Child Health and Human Development (NICHD). (2000). *Report of the National Reading Panel. Teaching children to read: An evidence-based assessment of the scientific research literature on reading and its implications for reading instruction: Reports of the sub-groups.* Available at *www.nichd.nig.gov/publications/nrp/report.htm.*

Nelson, J. R., Smith, D. J., & Dodd, J. M. (1992). The effects of teaching a summary skills strategy to students identified as learning disabled on their comprehension of science text. *Education and Treatment of Children, 15*(3), 228–243.

Newcomer, P. (1999). *Standardized Reading Inventory—2nd Edition (SRI–2).* Austin, TX: PRO-ED.

Newman, G. (2001–2002). Comprehension strategy gloves. *The Reading Teacher, 55,* 329–332.

Norton, M. (1959). *The borrowers afloat.* Orlando, FL: Harcourt.

O'Connor, R. E., & Jenkins, J. R. (1995). Improving the generalization of sound–symbol knowledge: Teaching spelling to kindergarten children with disabilities. *Journal of Special Education, 29,* 255–275.

O'Shea, L. J., Sindelar, P. T., & O'Shea, D. J. (1987). The effects of repeated readings and attentional cues on the reading fluency and comprehension of learning disabled readers. *Learning Disabilities Research, 2,* 103–109.

Ogle, D. M. (1986). K-W-L: A teaching model that develops active reading of expository text. *The Reading Teacher, 39,* 564–570.

Ogle, D. M. (1989). The know, want to know, learn strategy. In K. D. Muth (Ed.), *Children's comprehension of text: Research to practice* (pp. 205–233). Newark, DE: International Reading Association.

Ohlhausen, M. M., & Roller, C. M. (1988). The operation of text structure and content schemata in isolation and in interaction. *Reading Research Quarterly, 23,* 70–88.

Ortiz, A. A., & Wilkinson, C. Y. (1991). Assessment and intervention model for the bilingual exceptional student (AIM for the BESt). *Teacher Education and Special Education, 14,* 35–42.

Overton, T. (2003). *Assessing learners with special needs: An applied approach* (4th Edition). Upper Saddle River, NJ: Merrill.

Palincsar, A. S. (1986). The role of dialogue in providing scaffolded instruction. *Educational Psychologist, 21,* 73–98.

Palincsar, A. S., & Brown, A. L. (1984). The reciprocal teaching of comprehension-fostering and comprehension-monitoring activities. *Cognition and Instruction, 1,* 117–175.

Palincsar, A. S., & Brown, A. L. (1989). Classroom dialogues to promote self-regulated comprehension. In J. E. Brophy (Ed.), *Advances in Research on Teaching* (Vol. 1, pp. 35–71). Greenwich, CT: JAI Press.

Palincsar, A. S., Brown, A. L., & Martin, S. M. (1987). Peer interaction in reading comprehension instruction. *Educational Psychologist, 22,* 231–253.

Paris, A. H., & Paris, S. G. (2003). Assessing narrative comprehension in young children. *Reading Research Quarterly, 38,* 36–76.

Paris, S. G., & Oka, E. R. (1986). Children's reading strategies, metacognition, and motivation. *Developmental Review, 6,* 25–56.

Paris, S. G., Lipson, M. Y., & Wixson, K. K. (1983). Becoming a strategic reader. *Contemporary Educational Psychology, 8*(3), 293–316.

Paris, S. G., Wasik, B. A., & Turner, J. C. (1991). The development of strategic readers. In R. Barr, M. L. Kamil, P. B. Mosenthal, & P. D. Pearson (Eds.), *Handbook of reading research* (Vol. 2, pp. 609–640). New York: Longman.

Pearson, P. D., & Dole, J. A. (1987). Explicit comprehension instruction: A review of research and a new conceptualization of instruction. *Elementary School Journal, 88,* 151–165.

Pearson, P. D., & Fielding, L. (1991). Comprehension instruction. In R. Barr, M. L. Kamil, P. Mosenthal, & P. D. Pearson (Eds.), *Handbook of reading research* (Vol. 2, pp. 815–860). New York: Longman.

Perez, B. (1998). *Sociocultural contexts of language and literacy.* Mahwah, NJ: Erlbaum.

Perfetti, C. A. (1985). *Reading ability.* New York: Oxford University Press.

Perfetti, C. A., & Lesgold, A. M. (1977). Discourse comprehension and sources of individual differences. In P. A. Carpenter & M. A. Just (Eds.), *Cognitive processes in comprehension* (pp. 141–183). Hillsdale, NJ: Erlbaum.

Pike, K., & Salend, S. J. (1995). Authentic assessment strategies. *Teaching Exceptional Children, 28,* 15–20.

Polloway, E., Epstein, M., Polloway, C., Patton, J., & Ball, D. (1986). Corrective reading program: An analysis of effectiveness with learning disabled and mentally retarded students. *Remedial and Special Education, 7,* 41–47.

Pressley, M. (1998). Reading instruction that works: The case for balanced teaching. New York: Guilford Press.

Pressley, M. (2000). Comprehension instruction in elementary school: A quarter-century of research progress. In M. M. Taylor, M. F. Graves, & P. Can Den Broek (Eds.), *Reading for meaning: Fostering comprehension in middle grades* (pp. 32–51). New York: Teachers College Press.

Pressley, M. (2000). What should comprehension instruction be the instruction of? In M. Kamil, P. Mosenthal, P. Pearson, & R. Barr (Eds.), *Handbook of reading research* (Vol. 3, pp. 545–561). Mahwah, NJ: Erlbaum.

Pressley, M., & Afflerbach, P. (1995). *Verbal protocols of reading: The nature of constructively responsive reading.* Hillsdale, NJ: Erlbaum.

Pressley, M., Brown, R., El-Dinary, P. B., & Afflerbach, P. (1995). The comprehension instruction that students need: Instruction fostering constructively responsive reading. *Learning Disabilities Research and Practice, 10,* 215–224.

Pressley, M., & El-Dinary, P. B. (1997). What we know about translating comprehension-strategies instruction research into practice. *Journal of Learning Disabilities, 30,* 486–488.

Pressley, M., El-Dinary, P. B., Gaskins, I., Schuder, T., Bergman, J., Almasi, J., et al. (1992). Beyond direct explanation: Transactional instruction of reading comprehension strategies. *Elementary School Journal, 92*(5), 513–555.

Pressley, M., Gaskins, I., Cunicelli, E. A., Burdick, N. J., Schaub-Matt, M., Lee, D. S., et al. (1991). Strategy instruction at Benchmark School: A faculty interview study. *Learning Disability Quarterly, 14,* 19–48.

Pressley, M., & Hilden, K. R. (2006). Cognitive strategies: Production deficiencies and successful strategy instruction everywhere. In D. Kuhn & R. Siegler (Eds.) (W. Damon & R.

Lerner, Series Editors), *Handbook of child psychology, Vol. 2. Cognition, perception, and language* (6th ed., pp. 511–556). Hoboken NJ: Wiley.

Pressley, M., Hogan, K., Wharton-McDonald, R., & Mistretta, J. (1996). The challenges of instructional scaffolding: The challenges of instruction that supports student thinking. *Learning Disabilities Research and Practice, 11,* 138–146.

Pressley, M., Schuder, T., SAIL faculty and administration, Bergman, J. L., & El-Dinary, P. B. (1992). A researcher–educator collaborative interview study of transactional comprehension strategies instruction. *Journal of Educational Psychology, 84,* 231–246.

Pressley, M., Wood, E., Woloshyn, V.E., Marting, V., King, A., Menke, D. (1992). Encouraging mindful use of prior knowledge: Attempting to construct explanatory answers facilitates learning. *Educational Psychologist, 27,* 91–110.

Quezada, Y., Williams, E., & Flores, V. (2006). Inspiration outline of basic stages of reciprocal teaching. Retrieved March 16, 2006, from *http://condor.admin.ccny.cuny.edu/~yq6048/ basic1.jpg*

Rabren, K., Darch, C., & Eaves, R. C. (1999). The differential effects of two systematic reading comprehension approaches with students with learning disabilities. *Journal of Learning Disabilities, 32*(1), 36–47.

RAND Reading Study Group. (2002). *Reading for understanding: Towards an R&D program in reading comprehension.* Retrieved March 3, 2006, from *www.rand.org/multi/achievementforall/reading/readreport.html*

Raphael, T. (1986). Teaching question-and-answer relationships revisited. *The Reading Teacher, 37,* 377–382.

Raphael, T. E. (1986). Teaching question answer relationships, revisited. *The Reading Teacher, 39,* 516–522.

Rathvon, N. (2004). *Early reading assessment: A practitioner's handbook.* New York: Guilford Press.

Readence, J. E., Bean. T. W., & Baldwin, R. S. (1998). *Content area literacy: An integrated approach* (5th ed.). Dubuque, IA: Kendall/Hunt.

Reid, D. K., Hresko, P. W., & Hammill, D. D. (2001). *Test of Early Reading Ability—Third Edition.* Circle Pines, MN: AGS.

Richgels, D. J., McGee, L. M., & Slaton, E. A. (1989). Teaching expository text structure in reading and writing. In K. D. Muth (Ed.), *Children's comprehension of text* (pp. 167–184). Newark, DE: International Reading Association.

Riverside Publishing. (1994). *Riverside—Performance Assessment Series* (R-PAS). Itasca, IL: Author.

Riverside Publishing. (2005). *Batería III Woodcock–Muñoz: Pruebas de Aprovechamiento, Revisada.* Itasca, IL: Author.

Rogoff, B., & Gardner, W. P. (1984). Adult guidance of cognitive development. In B. Rogoff & J. Lave (Eds.), *Everyday cognition: Its development in social context* (pp. 95–116). Cambridge, MA: Harvard University Press.

Roller, C. (1996). *Variability not disability: Struggling readers in a workshop classroom.* Newark, DE: International Reading Association.

Rosenblatt, L. M. (1978). *The reader, the text, the poem: The transactional theory of the literary work.* Carbondale: Southern Illinois University Press.

Rosenblatt, L. M. (1983). *Literature as exploration* (4th ed.). New York: Modern Language Association of America.

Rosenshine, B., & Meister, C. (1994). Reciprocal teaching: A review of the research. *Review of Educational Research, 64,* 479–530.

Roth, F. P., & Speckman, N. J. (1986). Narrative discourse: Spontaneously generated stories of learning-disabled and normally achieving students. *Journal of Speech–Language–Hearing Pathology, 51,* 8–23.

Rowe, M. B. (1986). Wait time: Slowing down may be a way of speeding up! *Journal of Teacher Education, 37(1),* 43–50.

Salvia, J., & Ysseldyke, J. E. (2001). *Assessment* (8th ed.). Boston: Houghton Mifflin.

Sarroub, L., & Pearson, P. D. (1998). Two steps forward, three steps back: The stormy history of reading comprehension assessment. *Clearing House, 72,* 97–106.

Saskatchewan Learning. (2002). *English language arts: A curriculum guide for the elementary level.* Retrieved June 29, 2006, from *www.sasked.gov.sk.ca/docs/ela/assessment/p120.html*

Schumaker, J. B., Denton, P. H., & Deshler, D. D. (1984). *The paraphrasing strategy.* Lawrence, KA: University of Kansas.

Schumaker, J., Deshler, D., Alley, G., Warner, M., & Denton, P. (1984). Multipass: A learning strategy for improving reading comprehension. *Learning Disability Quarterly, 5,* 295–304.

Schumm, J. S., Moody, S. W., & Vaughn, S. R. (2000). Grouping for reading instruction: Does one size fit all? *Journal of Learning Disabilities, 33,* 477–488.

Scott, J. A., & Nagy, W. E. (2004). Developing word consciousness. In J. F. Baumann & E. J. Kame'enui (Eds.), *Vocabulary instruction: Research to practice* (pp. 201–217). New York: Guilford Press.

Seymour, J. R., & Osana, H. P. (2003). Reciprocal teaching procedures and principles: Two teachers' developing understanding. *Teaching and Teacher Education, 19,* 325–344.

Shannon, P., Kame'enui, E. J., & Baumann, J. F. (1988). An investigation of children's ability to comprehend character motives. *American Educational Research Journal. 25(3),* 441–462.

Shinn, M. R., & Bamonto, S. (1998). Advanced applications of curriculum-based measurement: "Big ideas" and avoiding confusion. In M. R. Shinn (Ed.), *Advanced applications of curriculum-based measurement* (pp. 1–31). New York: Guilford Press.

Simmons, D. C., & Kame'enui, E. (1998). *What reading research tells us about children with diverse learning needs: Bases and basics.* Mahwah, NJ: Erlbaum.

Simmons, D. C., Kame'enui, E. J., & Darch, C. B. (1988). The effect of textual proximity on fourth- and fifth-grade LD students' metacognitive awareness and strategic comprehension behavior. *Learning Disability Quarterly, 11(4),* 380–395.

Snow, C. E. (2002). *Reading for understanding: Toward a research and development program in reading comprehension.* Pittsburgh: RAND.

Snyder, L., Caccamise, D., & Wise, B. (2005). The assessment of reading comprehension: Considerations and cautions. *Topics in Language Disorders, 25,* 33–50.

Staal, L. A. (2000). The story face: An adaptation of story mapping that incorporates visualization and discovery learning to enhance reading and writing. *The Reading Teacher, 54,* 26–31.

Stahl, R. J. (1994). *Using "think-time" and "wait-time" skillfully in the classroom.* Bloomington, IN: ERIC Clearninghouse for Social Studies and Social Science Education. Available at *www.atozteacherstuff.com/pages/1884.shtml*

Stahl, S. A. (1999). *Vocabulary development.* Cambridge, MA: Brookline Books.

Stahl, S. A., & Stahl, K. A. D. (2004). Word wizards all! Teaching word meanings in preschool and primary education. In J. F. Baumann & E. J. Kame'enui (Eds.), *Vocabulary instruction: Research to practice* (pp. 59–80). New York: Guilford Press.

Stauffer, R. G. (1969). *Teaching reading as a thinking process.* New York: Harper & Row.

Stein, C., & Goldman, J. (1980). Beginning reading instruction for children with minimal brain dysfunction. *Journal of Learning Disabilities, 13,* 219–222.

Stein, N. L., & Nezworski, T. (1978). The effects of organization and instructional set on story memory. *Discourse Processes, 1*, 177–193.

Susskind, E. (1979). Encouraging teachers to encourage children's curiousity: A pivotal competence. *Journal of Clinical and Child Psychology, 8*, 101–106.

Swanson, H. L. (1999). Reading research for students with LD: A meta-analysis of intervention outcomes. *Journal of Learning Disabilities, 32*(6), 504–532.

Swanson, H. L. (2001). Reading intervention research outcomes and students with LD: What are the major instructional ingredients for successful outcomes? *Perspectives, 27*(2), 18–20.

Swanson, H. L., Hoskyn, M., & Lee, C. (1999). *Interventions for students with learning disabilities: A meta-analysis of treatment outcome.* New York: Guilford Press.

Taylor, B. M. (1982). A summarizing strategy to improve middle grade students' reading and writing skills. *The Reading Teacher, 36*, 202–205.

Texas Education Agency and University of Texas Center for Reading and Language Arts (2001). *Texas second grade teacher reading academy.* Austin, TX: Author.

Torgesen, J. K., & Licht, B. (1983). The learning disabled child as an inactive learner: Restrospect and prospects. In J. D. McKinney & L. Feagans (Eds.), *Current topics in learning disabilities* (Vol. 1, pp. 3–32). Norwood, NJ: Ablex.

Valcke, M. (2002). Cognitive load: Updating the theory? *Learning and Instruction, 12*, 147–154.

Vaughn, S., & Linan-Thompson, S. (2004). *Research-based methods of reading instruction: Grades K–3.* Alexandria, VA: Association for Supervision and Curriculum Development.

Vaughn, S., Bos, C., & Schumm, J. S. (2007). *Teaching students who are exceptional, diverse, and at risk in the general education classroom* (4th ed.). Boston: Allyn & Bacon.

Vaughn, S., Chard, D., Bryant, D. P., Coleman, M., Tyler, B., Thompson, S., et al. (2000). Fluency and comprehension interventions for third-grade students: Two paths to improved fluency. *RASE: Remedial and Special Education, 21*(6), 325–335.

Vaughn, S., Gersten, R., & Chard, D. (2000). The underlying message in LD intervention research: Findings from research syntheses. *Exceptional Children, 67*, 99–114.

Vaughn, S., Moody, S., & Schumm, J. S. (1998). Broken promises: Reading instruction in the resource room. *Exceptional Children, 64*, 211–226.

Vellutino, F. R., & Scanlon, D. M. (1987). Phonological coding, phonological awareness, and reading ability: Evidence from a longitudinal and experimental study. *Merrill–Palmer Quarterly, 33*, 321–363.

Venable, G. P. (2003). Confronting complex text: Readability lessons from students with language learning disabilities. *Topics in Language Disorders, 23*(3), 225–240.

Vygotsky, L. S. (1978). *Mind in society.* Cambridge, MA: Harvard University Press.

Wade, S. E., Buxton, W. M., & Kelly, M. (1999). Using think-alouds to examine reader-text interest. *Reading Research Quarterly, 34*, 194–216.

Walsh, J. A., & Sattes, B. D. (2005). *Quality questioning: Research-based practice to engage every learner.* Thousand Oaks, CA: Corwin Press.

Ward, L., & Traweek, D. (1993). Application of a metacognitive strategy to assessment, intervention, and consultation: A think-aloud technique. *Journal of School Psychology, 31*(4), 469–485.

Weaver, C. A., III, & Kintsch, W. (1991). Expository text. In R. Barr, M. L. Kamil, P. Mosenthal, & P. D. Pearson (Eds.), *Handbook of reading research* (Vol. 2, pp. 230–244. White Plains, NY: Longman.

Whaley, J. F. (1981). Story grammars and reading instruction. *The Reading Teacher, 34*, 762–771.

White, T. G., Sowell, J., & Yanagihara, A. (1989). Teaching elementary students to use word-part clues. *The Reading Teacher, 42*, 302–309.

Whitney, P., & Budd, D. (1996). Think-aloud protocols and the study of comprehension. *Discourse Processes, 21*(3), 341–351.

Wiederholt, J. L., & Blalock, G. (2000). *Gray Silent Reading Tests (GSRT)*. Austin, TX: PRO-ED.

Wiederholt, J. L., & Bryant, B. R. (1991). *Gray Oral Reading Test—Fourth Edition* (GORT-D-4). Austin, TX: PRO-ED.

Wiederholt, J. L., & Bryant, B. R. (2001). *Gray Oral Reading Test—4th Edition* (GORT-4). Austin, TX: PRO-ED.

Williams, J. P. (1988). Identifying main ideas: A basic aspect of reading comprehension. *Topics in Language Disorders, 8*(3), 1–13.

Williams, J. P. (1993). Comprehension of students with and without learning disabilities: Identification of narrative themes and idiosyncratic text representations. *Journal of Educational Psychology, 85*, 631–641.

Williams, J. P. (1998). Improving the comprehension of disabled readers. *Annals of Dyslexia, 48*, 213–238.

Williams, J. P. (2000). *Strategic processing of text: Improving reading comprehension for students with learning disabilities* (Report No. EDO-EC-00-8). Reston, VA: Council for Exceptional Children. (ERIC Document Reproduction Service No. ED 449596)

Williams, J. P. (2005). Instruction in reading comprehension for primary-grade students: A focus on text structure. *Journal of Special Education, 39*, 6–18.

Williams, J. P., Hall, K. M., & Lauer, K. D. (2004). Teaching expository text structure to young at-risk learners: Building the basics of comprehension instruction. *Exceptionality, 12*(3), 129–144.

Williams, K. T. (2001). *Group Reading Assessment and Diagnostic Evaluation* (GRADE). Circle Pines, MN: American Guidance Service.

Wong, B. Y. L., & Jones, W. (1982). Increasing metacomprehension in learning disabled and normally achieving students through self-questioning training. *Learning Disability Quarterly, 5*, 228–240.

Wood, E., Pressley, M., & Winne, P. H. (1990). Elaborative interrogation effects on children's learning of factual content. *Journal of Educational Psychology, 82*, 741–748.

Wood, P., Bruner, J., & Ross, G. (1976). The role of tutoring in problem solving. *Journal of Child Psychology and Psychiatry, 17*, 89–100.

Woodcock, R. W. (1998). *Woodcock Reading Mastery Test*. Circle Pines, MN: American Guidance Service.

Woods, L. M., & Moe, A. (1999). *Analytical Reading Inventory—Sixth Edition*. Columbus, OH: Merrill Education.

Wright, J. (2006). *Curriculum-based measurement: A manual for teachers*. Retrieved July 1, 2006, from *www.interventioncentral.org/download.php*

Index